THE WORLD OF
ELIZABETH GOUDGE

SYLVIA GOWER

Girls Gone By Publishers

Published by Girls Gone By Publishers
The Vicarage, Church Street, Coleford, Radstock, Somerset, BA3 5NG
www.ggbp.co.uk

First privately published by Periwinkle 2001
First published by Girls Gone By Publishers 2020; reprinted with
corrections 2021, reprinted 2023
Text © The Estate of Sylvia Gower
Text from the works of Elizabeth Goudge © the estate of Elizabeth
Goudge, reproduced with permission from David Higham Associates.
Publishers' Introduction and Books by Elizabeth Goudge © Girls Gone
    By Publishers 2020
Note on the Text © Alison Neale 2020
Design and Layout © Girls Gone By Publishers 2020

Cover design by Ken Websdale
Typeset in England by GGBP
Printed and bound by Short Run Press, Exeter

ISBN 978-1-84745-281-8

CONTENTS

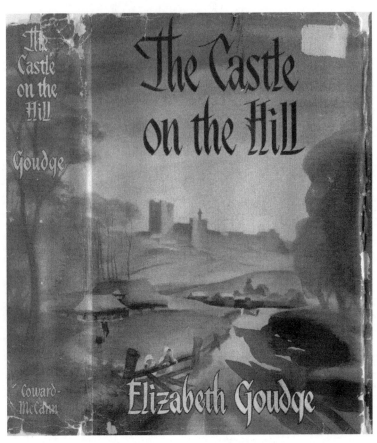

THE FIRST AMERICAN EDITION OF *THE CASTLE ON THE HILL*

PUBLISHERS' INTRODUCTION

SYLVIA GOWER, HITCHHIKING TO RYE ON 20 MAY 1950

In June this year (2020) Ann Mackie-Hunter suggested to me that we should republish Sylvia Gower's *The World of Elizabeth Goudge*. It had been first published in 2001, was almost impossible to get hold of (there was a copy on Amazon selling for over £900!) and it would go well with the four children's books we had already published: *Henrietta's House*, *The Sister of the Angels*, *The Valley of Song* and *Smoky-House*. We knew that Sylvia Gower had died on 13th December 2008 and asked Hilary Clare to track down the heir of the estate. To cut a long story short, this turned out to be Sylvia's husband, George, who is 92. He was delighted that we wanted to publish Sylvia's book, and gave immediate consent, sounding rather surprised when I insisted we sign a contract! George has been incredibly helpful, providing us with a number of Sylvia's books which we didn't own, and also with the photograph of Sylvia which you see here.

I should say that I absolutely agreed with Ann that to republish *The World of Elizabeth Goudge* (*WEG*) made very good sense, but I have to confess that it is Ann who is the real Elizabeth Goudge fan, not me. I don't actually like her books, and I had no intention of reading *WEG*. However, George told me that he didn't have the originals of the photographs Sylvia had used in *WEG*, and they had not come out well in the book. I looked at the chapter headings and asked on my Friday e-newsletter for pictures of those places. Quite understandably, a number of people asked things like, "but where in Devon?" It was no good, I was going to have to read *WEG*!

Read it I did. I could hardly put it down, and finished it in a couple of days. I was completely gripped from start to finish. I was then able to ask in a more sensible way for photographs and also for dustwrappers of some of Elizabeth Goudge's books. I have had a wonderful response. In a couple of cases, I asked two vicars (I am a vicar myself) and got terrific results.

When the Revd Andrew Bailey, Rector of Milton, took the photograph of the Goudge grave, it was found to be without its cross (see photographs on pages 92 and 115). We decided that we should organise a Just Giving page in order to raise funds to have a new cross put on the grave. If you are interested in contributing to that, please go to the Elizabeth Goudge page on our website, www. ggbp.co.uk/authors-and-series/elizabeth-goudge/, and you will find the details. If you would like to donate but are unable to do this yourself, please do not send any money to GGBP but ask a friend or relative to donate on the Just Giving page for you.

There were some illustrations we could not find again, and so have used the original ones from *WEG*. Ken Websdale, who attends to our covers, has done the best job he can with them, but at this stage I don't know how well they will come out. Where this is the case, in the caption I have said that the photograph was used in the first edition of *WEG*. There are a couple of photographs that were used in the first edition which I have been able to source from elsewhere and I have indicated these by adding 'new scan'. Otherwise, all illustrations are new for this book. Some have been taken from old postcards (either emailed to me, or bought from eBay), but many photographs were emailed to me by people who have gone specially to take them, and in some cases driven miles to do so. Dustwrappers have been emailed by various people, and Hilary Boulton, who lives close by, has driven over on several occasions, following a frantic telephone call from me, and happily left her books with me so that I could scan the wrappers at my convenience. Some wrappers I have found on the internet, and managed to save at the correct level of dpi (don't ask!) for reproduction in this book.

In her Note on the Text (see page 11), Alison Neale has written about the text, but I should also like to say that we have added three chapters – this Introduction, the Note on the Text, and a second list of Books by Elizabeth Goudge. When Sylvia compiled her list (pages 259–261), she did not have access to the internet in the same way that we do now. It seemed sensible, for clarity's sake, to add this new list – and I have to confess to being curious myself. We have also added a Family Tree – this was prepared by Alison Neale and includes information supplied by Christine Woodall in Guernsey.

On our back cover, you will see the blue plaque on Rose Cottage, Peppard Common – Elizabeth Goudge's final home. It was Sylvia Gower who was really instrumental in this being put up.

There are a lot of people who have helped in different ways, and I thank them now. I have only included what they have done where they have taken particular photographs. I list them in alphabetical order.

Revd Andrew Bailey, Pat Barker, Rachel Best, Gill Bilski, John Blamey, Rene Blamey (Devon photographs), Elizabeth Boardman (Oxford photographs), Hilary Boulton, Helen Burner, Ann Butcher, Hilary Clare (Wells pictures by E W Haslehurst), Lalage Clay, Sonja

Crosby, Alison Dennis (Ely photographs), Kerryn Dixon-Ward, Barbara Dryden, Adrianne Fitzpatrick, Jo Fletcher, George Gower, Pat Hanby, Hilary Hartley, Laura Hicks, Jennifer Hill, Mia Jha, Ruth Jolly, Jana Jopson, Beth Lamb, Samantha Little, Moira Lott, Christine MacDonald (Buckler's Hard photograph), Alison Neale, Revd Deborah Parsons, Mhairead Robertson, Betty Rylance, Lorna Sharpe, Andrea Smith, Julia Smith, Julianne Stein, Nicky Wade, Ken Websdale, Helen White (Peppard photographs) and Christine Woodall (Guernsey photographs).

THE FIRST EDITION OF *A CITY OF BELLS*

A RATHER RACY AMERICAN EDITION

THE EDITION OF *THE LITTLE WHITE HORSE* WAS INCLUDED IN THE FIRST
EDITION OF THIS BOOK (NEW SCAN)

NOTE ON THE TEXT

In republishing *The World of Elizabeth Goudge* we have used the text of the first and only edition of the book.

We have standardised the presentation of the text to reflect both other GGBP titles and also non-fiction publishing in general, including the layout of the pages and chapter titles, the presentation of book titles in italics rather than quotation marks, the use of [square brackets] for insertions into quotations made by Sylvia Gower, and the use of UK rules on punctuation around quotation marks.

The high number of illogical spelling mistakes in the original book suggests that a typed paper manuscript might have been scanned to create the first edition and never subsequently proofread. We have corrected obvious typos, and also standardised inconsistencies, such as titles of jobs and organisations, to match the author's majority usage. We have amended apostrophe use throughout.

A team of proofreaders, fact checkers, local experts and fans of Elizabeth Goudge's work has pored over the text. Names of real people and places, literary characters and locations have been checked and corrected where necessary. Where possible, quotations have been compared to the original sources and edited to match. Mentions of Elizabeth Goudge's books have been standardised to the title of the first edition (unless within a quotation); publishers and publication dates have been checked. The bibliography at the back of the book has been corrected accordingly, and a new, expanded bibliography has been added which includes a few publications mentioned in the text but not previously listed there, US titles where they differ, alternative titles to the UK editions, and a few film and television adaptations that might be of interest.

The book was written nearly twenty years ago, and while we did not wish to update the text to reflect changes to the world in 2020 and new information that has come to light, there were a few occasions where we felt that some additional information might be of interest, or come in useful to anyone following in Sylvia Gower's footsteps. Therefore, we have added a few new footnotes, marked as follows:

†   first footnote in a chapter
††   second footnote in a chapter
‡   third footnote in a chapter
‡‡   fourth footnote in a chapter
§   fifth footnote in a chapter

The author's original footnotes still use an asterisk.* If the reference to a footnote has ⁿᵖ after it, that means that the footnote itself appears on the following page.

We have been careful only to make changes for accuracy and clarification; we have not altered the text based on our personal preference or style. *The World of Elizabeth Goudge* is still essentially as Sylvia Gower wrote it, and we sincerely hope we have not allowed any new errors to creep in.

Alison Neale

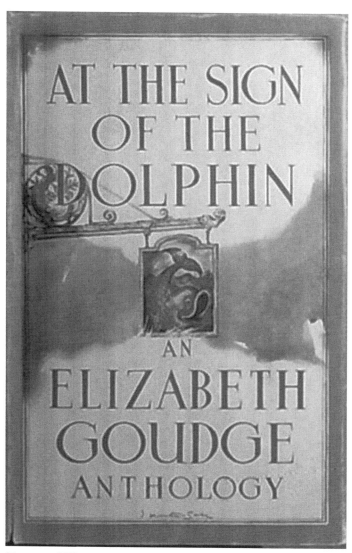

THE FIRST UK EDITION OF *AT THE SIGN OF THE DOLPHIN*, ORIGINALLY PUBLISHED IN THE US AS *THE ELIZABETH GOUDGE READER*

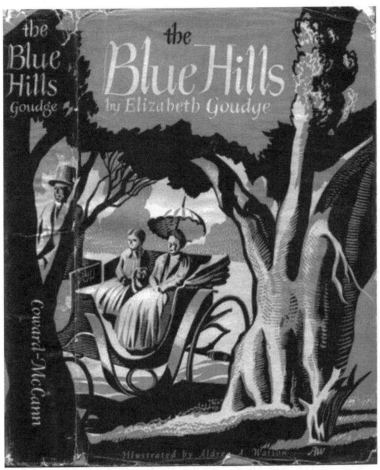

THE SECOND IMPRESSION OF THE FIRST EDITION OF *THE BLUE HILLS*
(US TITLE OF *HENRIETTA'S HOUSE*)

CONTENTS

THE FIRST EDITION OF *THE WORLD OF ELIZABETH GOUDGE*

INTRODUCTION

During the 1950s and 1960s news would spread between enthusiastic readers: 'There's a new Elizabeth Goudge book out, have you read it?'

Sure enough on the next visit to the local book shop, there, prominently displayed, they would see a picture of a grey-haired, gentle, gracious lady, surrounded by pristine copies of her latest book.

The more affluent would hand over their cash and hurry out of the shop with a warm glow of anticipation—they had just acquired a book guaranteed to lift them out of their mundane routine and to some perhaps give a boost to the vague sense of spiritual starvation.

Others, to whom buying books was a rare luxury, would reluctantly decide they had best try the library and hopefully scan the G section on their next visit. Fortunately libraries were better funded in that era, when there were no tapes or videos to compete for the available money, and our readers had a good chance of being lucky, and quickly removing it from the shelf before someone else beat them to it.

Elizabeth's books were eagerly awaited by readers in Europe and in the USA, as well as in the British Isles. Some overseas publishers would change the title of the book, causing some confusion to today's readers.

Fortunately for today's seekers of her books, millions of her books were sold worldwide, many of them reprinted several times, often as paperbacks, so that until recently her books could easily be found new, or in good second-hand book shops.

The situation is changing, until now some readers have to use booksearch services to find ones they want, and quite high prices are being asked because of their increasing rarity. When I first started my research for this book I rather expected to only find Elizabeth's books remembered by older readers, so it was a pleasant surprise to find admirers of her work from various age groups. One librarian told me her parents had bought her the children's books, which she had so much loved she went on to the rest as she got older. A newspaper editor, avid for books, had first read books belonging to his parents, and then went on to find more. In one charity book shop, the assistant, herself a fan, told me they were so often asked for her books, they put any that came in straight into a box of their own.

An Italian student studying at Florence University contacted me to say she was writing her thesis on the historical writing of Elizabeth Goudge.

All these and many more agreed with me that Elizabeth Goudge's writing should not be allowed to fade from the world of books without some record being made of her achievements. Unfortunately, with the commercialism in today's publishing world, it is hard to stem the flow of worthwhile books disappearing for ever. The aim of this book is to remind readers of the unique contribution she made to literature, and even hopefully introduce it to a few more before it is too late.

To those readers who have read all or some of Elizabeth's books, including *The Joy of the Snow*, I have to ask for understanding if they find some parts repetitive. To any who haven't any previous knowledge of her writing, I must ask for tolerance that I have only been able to give sketchy summaries of the books, hoping their appetites may be whetted to want to read the books and find out more for themselves.

I have to confess that my first reading of Elizabeth's books years ago was somewhat haphazard, so to read them again in the right sequence made for even more enjoyment. It made me want to 'follow in her footsteps' as I was aware many other readers had already done at the height of her popularity.

As with any 'pilgrimage', I found my journeys gave me a much deeper understanding of the influence places can have on the writer's material, and so I felt I would like to also share this with other admirers of Elizabeth's work, who for various reasons might never get a chance to visit these places for themselves.

Elizabeth often expressed her gratitude for having lived in so many lovely places. I too am grateful for it, enabling me to not only visit them, but also meet so many helpful people who still enjoy living in those lovely places.

Sylvia Gower
December 2001

ELIZABETH GOUDGE AND HER MOTHER IN DEVON

TOWER HOUSE, WELLS (USED IN THE FIRST EDITION OF *WEG*)

THE EARLY YEARS PART 1

WELLS 1900–1911

No child can have lived in lovelier homes than my first two homes, or in a more enchanted city than Wells at the beginning of the century.

For over three centuries, Tower House, in the small cathedral city of Wells in Somerset, is thought to have been home to successive precentors of the cathedral.

The precentor is the man in charge of the music and liturgy in the cathedral and is one of the five dignitaries who handle the day-to-day affairs of the cathedral. The proximity of Tower House to Vicars' Close and to the cathedral would have made it a very suitable home for the holder of this important position. Possibly the responsibility the post brought with it made one of its holders in the 16th century decide he needed an occasional bolt-hole, as the tower which gave the house its name was added to the existing 14th-century building.

However, by the late 19th century the role of the house had changed and it was assigned as a home for the vice-principal of the theological college which had opened in the Old Archdeaconry in 1890. When this post was filled by the Reverend Henry Goudge, Tower House became the first married home for him and his new wife, the former Miss Ida Collenette from Guernsey. On April 24th, 1900 a daughter was born there and given the name Elizabeth after her late paternal grandmother.

The Goudge family continued living in Wells until 1911. Writing seventy years later about her childhood there, Elizabeth said: 'No child can have lived in lovelier homes than my first two homes, or in a more enchanted city than Wells at the beginning of the century.' This chapter sets out to consider what part those formative years played towards making her a successful novelist. Her second novel, *A City of Bells*, published in 1936, and a children's book, *Henrietta's House*, in 1942, both used her memories of living in Wells, although she gave her fictional cathedral city the name of Torminster.†

Elizabeth acknowledged that she saw those years in Wells from a fairly privileged viewpoint. With her father's salary around £500 a year, they were able to afford the services of a nanny, three maids, and a gardener.

Looking back on her childhood, she always said that she was grateful she was born when she was, in a more peaceful era, before the coming of the motor car. It could well have been the remembrance of those safe, motor-free days that led her to write the very amusing episode in *Henrietta's House* about the first car ever seen in Torminster: 'The peace of Torminster Cathedral Close had been broken by the most peculiar roaring sound, interrupted now and then by clankings and grindings like a goods train shunting, and pops and bangs like a cannon going off, while there drifted upon the summer breeze a most unpleasant oily smell that quite overwhelmed the scent of the flowers in the Close gardens … There was a terrifying hoot and through the archway came clanging and banging a scarlet dragon belching white smoke, and perched on top of it were three people with huge heads and great goggling eyes like giant frogs …'

Needless to say, in the story the owners abandoned the monstrosity, but the era of the motor car was to be unstoppable in Wells as elsewhere. No wonder, like many of her generation,

† *Henrietta's House* was published in the USA as *The Blue Hills*.

THE PRINCIPAL'S HOUSE, WELLS
(USED IN THE FIRST EDITION OF *WEG*, NEW SCAN)
LOOKING DOWN ST ANDREW'S STREET TOWARDS THE CATHEDRAL,
THE WAY ELIZABETH WOULD HAVE WALKED FROM HER HOME,
SHOWING THE CHAIN GATE

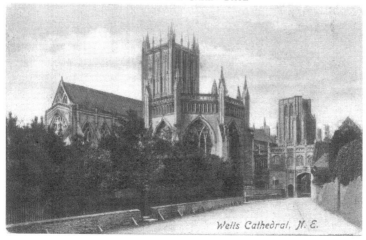

Wells Cathedral, N. E.

Elizabeth looked back on a quieter world with some nostalgia. Neither she nor her father ever drove a car, though, with her love of adventure, if she had not become a semi-invalid after Elizabeth's birth, Mrs Goudge might well have liked to do so. Mrs Goudge's invalidity, thought to have been the result of a cycling accident before the birth, was naturally to have its impact too on Elizabeth's life.

The promotion of the Reverend Goudge as principal at the theological college, meant that when Elizabeth was three years old, the family moved just across the road to another medieval house with the garden adjoining that of the Bishop's Palace. Both her homes were in the area known as 'The Liberty', where at that time, all the houses were occupied by church officials. Today many of them, including Tower House, are in private ownership.

Elizabeth referred to her second home as 'The Principal's House', but it is now known as 'The Rib' and is the residence of the headmaster of the Cathedral School.†† She seems to have remembered it best for the path in the garden that led her to the cloisters and to the palace itself where she would visit the kindly Mrs Kennion, the Bishop's wife, in the Long Gallery. She used the Long Gallery as the setting for the Bishop's annual Christmas party given to the choirboys in *A City of Bells*, and wrote of it: 'Few lovelier rooms were to be met with at this time in England than the gallery of the Bishop's Palace at Torminster—it stretched the whole length of one wing of the palace and was perfectly proportioned for its length.'

The palace is still the official residence of the present Bishop of Wells and Bath, but a part of it is now open to the public at certain times, including the Long Gallery.

Elizabeth also recalled the wells in the grounds which had given the city its name. They caused dampness in the house to the

†† The house was sold in 2016 and is now a private residence.

detriment of the health of its residents—possibly including her own as she was later disabled with arthritis.

By having Grandfather and Grandmother Fordyce in *A City of Bells* living in Tower House, though calling it 'Number One, The Close', she made it the more familiar of the two houses to her readers—possibly because she also remembered it better. After her father's promotion, the position of vice-principal was given to his friend, Arthur Hollis, later to be Bishop of Taunton. Elizabeth became very friendly with the Hollis family and continued spending time with them in her old home. She remembered Mrs Hollis reading stories to a group of children in the panelled drawing room, particularly a story called, 'The Cocky Olley Bird' ‡, which influenced her years later when writing *The Bird in the Tree*.

She recalled being taken by the two older Hollis boys to visit the third baby boy when he was a week old, and her subsequent disappointment when no new baby came to their household. The Hollis boys became her main playmates in those early years as well as sharing lessons with her. Not surprisingly she learnt the art of climbing trees from them, even though she sometimes got stuck until her shrieks brought the gardener to the rescue.

When the family moved from Wells Elizabeth was lonely for the first time in her life and admitted 'she wept bitterly, always being a watery child'. I had often speculated how frequently a red-haired, freckled boy appeared in her books, so it was now possible to surmise she was remembering one of her early playmates. It would be interesting to know if she followed their fortunes in later life.

It appears that Elizabeth was consoled for the loss of her playmates by being allowed to ride on a borrowed Shetland pony, as well as acquiring numerous pets. Her mother's gift for storytelling seems to have initiated Elizabeth's earliest literary efforts as she remembered one story about Red Indians being told to her in daily instalments, which she later retold, with embellishments, to her

‡ The Cocky Olley Bird is actually the title, and a main character, in *The Cockyolly Bird* (1900), by Mabel Jessie Dearmer, who wrote and illustrated it

small friends. This seems to have given her the idea for producing a monthly magazine for them until the interest waned, while another spate of writing was abandoned in remorse for not feeding her caterpillars due to absorption in her work. Fortunately for us, this was not to have a permanent effect on her desire to write.

Her education at this time was provided by a governess—Miss Lavington. Elizabeth later used her as the fictional Miss Lavender, although she said the former was a much stricter teacher, managing to teach her reluctant pupil 'the times tables and the dates of the kings and queens of England'.

I think that 'the enchanted city' did give this sensitive and imaginative child a secure and happy start in life—one that was to stand her in good stead in her work as a writer. In 1901 the population of Wells was 4,063, but by the time she wrote her autobiography in 1974 it had more than doubled to 8,855. Elizabeth kept in touch with friends in Wells for many years, but there is no evidence that she ever revisited it after moving away in 1911, so when writing the two books, she was relying on early memories, and her photographic mind to recreate the cathedral city of the 1900s. Of all the places I was later to visit she had used in her writing, it was at Wells I could follow most easily 'in her footsteps'.

Owing to the axing of the railways by Mr Beeching in the 1960s, it is no longer possible to arrive in Wells, as Elizabeth remembered doing, 'on the slow train that went puffing in and out between the hills'. The 'winding lanes' through which they went 'driving in a pony cart' are now roads linking the city with the M5. But as someone with no pre-car memories to be shattered, I still found it a magical experience to arrive in Wells on a lovely spring day and see the delightful old houses of this small market town, surrounded by the Mendip Hills—to visit the glorious cathedral, and the other ancient buildings that make it so special.

I had planned my visit in the spring as that was the time of year when Elizabeth in her books had described Jocelyn's, and later Henrietta's, first arrival at the city. Smelling the same spring flowers— hyacinths, red wallflowers and forget-me-nots, as they had done gave an evocative start to my visit. I felt that just as later Elizabeth associated Ely with the autumn season, so she had remembered Wells best in the spring. With her birthday at that time of the year, special birthday treats may have reinforced those memories.

Following directions to reach my first destination of 'Tower House', I had to stay very resolute not to stop at the other interesting places en route before passing under the ancient gateway known as 'The Chain Gate'.

For many years Tower House had remained a church property, eventually being used to accommodate theological students, during which time the house had been divided up into smaller rooms. After the college had moved to Salisbury in 1971, it had been put on the open market and bought by the present owner and her late husband. Being a keen reader of Elizabeth's books had been an extra inducement for Mrs Egan when purchasing the house. Since living at Tower House, she had become even more interested in Elizabeth's writing and was often called on to give talks about her to local groups. It was at her kind invitation I was privileged to visit the house where Elizabeth was born.

As I went up and down the road looking for the entrance to the house, I remembered Elizabeth writing that 'the house gave the impression of being impregnable' before deciding that the blue gate set unobtrusively in tall surrounding walls was the only possible way in. The dampness of the day made the gate reluctant to admit me to the private world inside, but it finally gave way to my persuasive pushing.

Once inside I was given a warm welcome and led into the house down a flight of stairs into a hall which felt just as Elizabeth had written, 'like going into a cave'. From there my hostess and her two dogs led me into a large, hospitable kitchen, where she told me something of her life in the house. The first task on moving there had been to restore the rooms to their original proportions, using materials as like the originals as possible. Over the years modern conveniences had been added but in keeping with the rest of the house. If Elizabeth could see it now I think she would feel very much at home, though more comfortable.

I was then shown over the house, going through the present drawing room which is thought to be the room in which Elizabeth had been born—then the dining room, not now as dim as in the days of candlelight described by Jocelyn. Going through a series of rooms and passages to reach the staircase leading to the tower, I was reminded of Jocelyn's experience in *A City of Bells* when searching for the missing children: 'finding anything in this house was not easy, for it seemed to have no geographical plan. Odd flights of steps ended at locked doors, twisting passages with wavy floors led apparently nowhere, and it was not until he had been barking his shins on sharp corners for ten minutes that Jocelyn opened a door leading into a spiral stone staircase that evidently wound up from the kitchen regions to the top of the tower.' Fortunately for me, the sharp corners are now thoughtfully lit by electric light.

The climb to the tower was more than compensated by the private view that one gets of Wells, looking over the stone parapet. I wondered when Elizabeth wrote of how on hot, stuffy nights, early in their marriage, her parents would drag their mattresses up there, whether she ever considered the possibility she could have been conceived up there. She always said that 'she loved high places'.

On the way down, I was shown into 'the angel room', where recently there had been an exciting discovery. Carrying out repairs before decorating, a workman had found a suspicious bulge on the wall by the window and asked permission to explore it further. A small piscina had been revealed, and this together with the little angel figure high up on one wall, had led experts to think the room had formerly been the precentor's private chapel.

Talking about Elizabeth's connections with Wells, my hostess related how she had been told by an elderly lady that she could remember the Dean who lived there in the early 1900s. She had little doubt that this was the Dean who Elizabeth confessed she had embellished when creating her fictional Dean in her book, describing him as: 'tall and handsome, with white mutton whiskers, a high pitched voice, and a top hat a little on the side; a wealthy man who drove his dog cart in a dashing manner and had an eye for horseflesh and pretty women.'

Elizabeth was very contrite after her father recognised the Dean in her book and was extremely angry with her, but the old lady confirmed that the real Dean 'had been very much a lady's man, and one to be kept at a distance'. It certainly gives an early example of Elizabeth's gift for observing characters, even though she took care to disguise them better in her writing. As I left Tower House I noticed there was still a mulberry tree growing near the entrance, and down the other end of the long garden there was a cedar 'towering against the sky, like a blue black mountain'.

Retracing my way back to the cathedral I now had time to stop at the external face of the famous cathedral clock and watch the antics of the figures known as Quarter Jacks as they struck the bell with their halberds. The clock, first mentioned in 1392, is thought to have been made to help the canons, who lived opposite in Vicars' Close, be punctual for services. It would have been part of Elizabeth's early life in Wells, so it's no wonder that Sarah, the cook in the Fordyce household, was depicted as carrying out her domestic duties to the chimes of the cathedral clock.

Being so young, the beauty of the cathedral and its services may not have had as much spiritual impact on Elizabeth as Ely Cathedral was to have later, but the many references to it prove how strong her memories remained with her through the years. When writing about Henrietta's visit there with Grandfather, one can't help thinking that she may have been remembering having similar thoughts: '[I]n spite of her grief [the sudden disappearance of Ferranti] she thrilled a little, as she always did, to its grandeur and loveliness ... Great pillars stood in ordered ranks all the way up the nave, so tall that it gave one a crick in the neck to look up to the place where their straightness curved into lovely dim arching shapes that went up and up into the roof and criss-crossed high over your head like the branches of trees in a forest.'

Were the ideas she made Henrietta express about God how she remembered her own at the same age? 'Her ideas about God were at this time extremely hazy but correct as far as they went. He lived in the Cathedral, she imagined, much as Grandfather lived in Number Two the Close, and was kind and good like Grandfather, only more so. He had made her, so she understood, and provided her with her dinner daily so as to perpetuate His work, and He must be great and beautiful because His house was like that.'

Attending Evensong on Easter Day at the cathedral, I couldn't help recalling (perhaps rather irreverently) the account in *A City of Bells* of the procession at the Patronal Festival, when the combined ages of the clergy in the procession was 484 years, making the Dean feel 'exactly like a—er—nursemaid'.

There was so much of interest to be seen in Wells, but my main purpose was to seek out the places that Elizabeth had used in her writing.

In the market square I had been told to look for a little gabled 'Hans Christian Andersen type' house. It was wedged between The Crown Inn and another tall building, and is now part of The Crown Inn. It is now known as The Penn Bar, because the Quaker William Penn is reputed to have preached from its upper windows. When Elizabeth lived in Wells it was known as The Royal Oak. My interest in it lay in the belief that it is the building where Elizabeth visualised Gabriel Ferranti living, and later in the story Jocelyn and Felicity. It certainly seemed to fit the description she gave: 'Between the tall Green Dragon and the equally tall bakery two doors off was wedged a little house only two stories high. Its walls were plastered and pale pink in colour and its gabled roof was tiled with wavy tiles and ornamented with cushions of green moss …' I was interested to discover that 'the tall bakery' had been a photographic shop during the early 1900s and that the owner, Mr Phillips, had taken many early photographs of interesting places and events in Wells at that time. Some of these can still be seen in a book about Wells by Tony Scrase.

One photograph shows a mayoral procession leaving the market place in 1903 and in the foreground a small girl is being held up by her nanny to get a better view. The nanny is dressed in the uniform of a Norland's nurse, so it is quite possible the small girl could have been Elizabeth.

Other photographs record events and places Elizabeth would have known. There is a rather grand grocer called 'Provision Importers', while the one of Taylor's the butchers shows the removable windows that were necessary before refrigeration was in use. There is also a photograph of a grand dress shop called 'Madame Rea' where elegant dresses were on display.

Would Elizabeth have seen the streets decorated for Edward the Seventh's coronation as another showed? Or the Empire Day celebrations as in another?

Troops are shown assembled outside the cathedral wearing the wide-brimmed hats of the soldiers who fought in the Boer War. Elizabeth would have heard much talk about the Boer War and this is apparent in the way she writes of Jocelyn's invalidity from that war at the beginning of *A City of Bells*.

Back in the Town Square I found the Town Hall where Elizabeth may have been taken to see the procession arrive for the Assizes, and also where we know she was taken to performances of *Merrie England* and '*The Pirates of Penzance*, amid potted plants on the platform'.

Where Martha and Mary's shop stood in the Market Square there are now craft shops, but with half-closed eyes, it's possible to imagine their shop 'with glass jars of coloured sweets, striped sticks of peppermint rock, and families of white sugar mice and pigs with pink noses and string tails'. It's very likely that like so many of her generation, Elizabeth was allowed too many sweets to be good for her teeth, and many dreaded visits to the dentist by so many characters in her stories suggest that she too suffered from dental troubles through the years.

In Sadler Street, just off the square, I found it easy to imagine the house where dear Miss Lavender had lived and practised her methods of self-education with the children. To get to the Bishop's Palace, I had to pass under another ancient gateway known as 'The Bishop's Eye'. The earliest part of the palace had been built in 1230 by Bishop Jocelyn and his name featured so much in the history of Wells that it is not surprising Elizabeth used it for the central character in her book about Torminster. Jocelyn had a brother Hugh, so again there was a ready-made name to give the irrepressible eight year old with his look of perpetual enquiry (and with red hair and freckles).

I had to see the moat and drawbridge to the palace which, because of the swans who pull the bellrope asking to be fed, is a magnet to all visitors to Wells. The descendants of the swans Elizabeth would have known still perform for today's visitors.

Many delightful dogs appear in Elizabeth's books, and the name given to the one living in Torminster was 'Mixed Biscuits'. His favourite walk was by the moat so that he could bark at the swans.

On the other side of the Cathedral Green was another building of interest—'The Old Deanery', now used as diocesan offices,‡ap but remembered by readers of *A City of Bells* as the place Felicity visited the Dean, hoping to persuade him to part with a substantial sum to back Jocelyn's play in London. After giving what he considered a generous contribution, the Dean was outraged when the Bishop, who had dropped by, also wrote Felicity a cheque (which the Dean makes it his business to see), for twice the amount of the Dean's, 'even though only last week when he had dined with the Bishop, he had been given Lemon not Dover Soles'.

Felicity was staying with her eccentric aunt at a house in The Liberty at that time. This aunt sounds to me like someone Elizabeth remembered from her years at Wells: 'she wore dresses in the colours of the Church's seasons … purple in Lent, red at Whitsun, white during festivals and green the rest of the year.' The same lady was said to have kept four parrots, one in each corner of her sitting room.

Parrots were often to feature in several of Elizabeth's later stories and must have been quite a popular pet at the time, being brought back by sailors from lands they had visited.

My journey to places associated with Elizabeth's early years would not have been complete without including some of the lovely countryside near to Wells. 'Driving picnics' were a very popular outing and she always remembered being taken by the Dean and his daughter to the Cheddar Gorge: 'It was a magnificent and electrifying experience. To this day I can see the high polished dog cart and hear the creak of the harness as the Dean drove slowly down the precipitous place. He must have been a skilful driver, for as he drove, he talked to his daughter far above my head. I heard their voices as though two enthroned Olympian Gods spoke to each other from cloud to cloud across blue air.'

When I visited the Cheddar Gorge it was a bank holiday and I doubt whether the Dean or his passengers could ever have imagined the crowds that would throng there nearly a century after that drive.

---

‡ The building was for sale in 2020, the diocesan offices having moved to modern accomodation.

Fortunately, away from the tourist spots I still found places as unspoilt as when Elizabeth rode her pony on the green turf above Tor Woods.

My visit to Wells had given me a glimpse into the serenity Elizabeth had imbibed from her early years there, and which she managed to impart to her readers in *A City of Bells* and *Henrietta's House*.

PENNILESS GATE, WELLS BY E W HASLEHURST, R.B.A. ELIZABETH WOULD HAVE WALKED THROUGH HERE TO THE MARKET PLACE

THE 'BISHOP'S EYE' BY E W HASLEHURST, R.B.A.
LOOKING FROM THE CATHDRAL GREEN INTO SADLER STREET

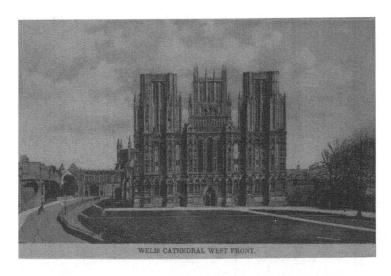

WELLS CATHEDRAL WEST FRONT.

THE CATHEDRAL TAKEN C 1920 WITH ST ANDREW'S STREET AND THE
DEANERY ON THE LEFT
THE THEOLOGICAL COLLEGE IN ST ANDREW'S STREET
BEFORE THE CHAIN GATE

THE DEANERY, TAKEN FROM THE GARDEN,
WITH THE CATHEDRAL ON THE LEFT
ST ANDREW'S STREET WITH THE CATHEDRAL ON THE RIGHT (NORTH SIDE)
LOOKING TOWARDS THE CHAPTER HOUSE AND CHAIN GATE

THE OZANNE WINDMILL, PARISH OF ST MARTIN'S, GUERNSEY

THE EARLY YEARS PART 2

GUERNSEY 1901–1914

Guernsey is a small island and the inhabitants of those days knew it like the palm of their hand. Yet to visit a favourite bay or clifftop six miles away for the fiftieth time brought no sense of stalemate. It was a visit to a well loved friend and always there was something new to see.

Elizabeth went on her first visit to the island when she was a year old. After Elizabeth's birth Mrs Goudge's health never permitted her to return to her old home ever again. The sea passage from Weymouth to St Peter Port was considered too gruelling an experience for her to undertake—the small steam ships of those days and the rough seas round the Channel Islands often made the journey an ordeal for the passengers. The area was notorious for shipwrecks on the treacherous rocks—a subject Elizabeth used later in dramatic events in her books.

Luckily for Elizabeth, her Guernsey aunts, Marie, Irene or Emily, were able to take her to visit her grandparents, Adolphus and Marie-Louise Collenette, every summer until the outbreak of the First World War.

The Collenette family, while paying allegiance to the British Crown, were proud of their Norman ancestry. By the time Elizabeth went there the family were speaking English with a French accent, though earlier they would have been French speaking. Many islanders at that time still spoke in the local patois. Elizabeth remembered hearing the patois spoken in the market or by the older islanders.† Her mother probably remained bilingual and it is likely that Elizabeth's French was quite good, as a French journalist interviewing her in the 1960s noticed that Elizabeth had understood her when she had lapsed into her native tongue at one point in the conversation.

Elizabeth adored her yearly visits to Guernsey where she could enjoy the same kind of carefree life her mother had known in her childhood. There were unspoilt bays and beaches for bathing and picnics; caves to explore and cliffs to climb. The lovely water lanes of the island, streams running down to the sea by the side of stony paths, under a canopy of ferns, were tempting to explore. There were the island specialities to be tasted—local shellfish, gâche cakes and Guernsey biscuits, purchasing some to take home for her mother at the end of her stay.

It was all such a contrast to her rather orderly upbringing in Wells and must surely have helped nurture the imaginative quality that was later to make her such a successful writer. Although sadly these visits were cut short when she was eleven years old, her memories of the island would have been kept fresh by her mother's stories and recollections of her childhood there.

Elizabeth's first novel, *Island Magic*, published in 1934 and dedicated to her mother, was based on Mrs Goudge's memories of events in her childhood.†† [np] Much of it, Elizabeth said in her autobiography, was written in the corner of her mother's bedroom when they were staying at their holiday cottage in Barton. Mrs Goudge had periods of illness, so it is possible to imagine Elizabeth keeping her company and helping her feel better by recalling happy childhood memories.

† Guernésiais is no longer considered a patois, but instead a separate language. In August 2020 the States of Guernsey announced a number of measures intended to halt and reverse the decline in its use.

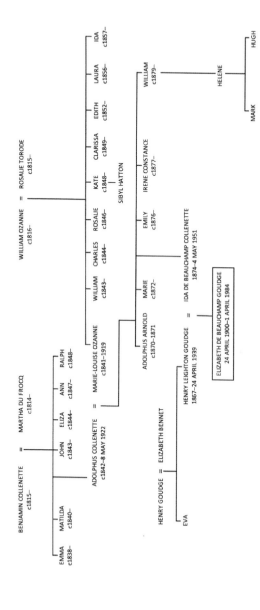

We thought that Elizabeth's family tree might be of interest when reading the early chapters of *The World of Elizabeth Goudge*. This tree contains all the family members mentioned in the biography. Where exact dates or ancestors' names were not given in the book, we have inserted these using Census records. For this reason, there are only approximate years of birth and few death dates. It is not intended to be an exhaustive rendition of EG's family, but instead a simple visual aid for the reader.

A LATER IMPRESSION OF THE FIRST EDITION DUSTWRAPPER OF
ISLAND MAGIC

They had moved to Devon when *Green Dolphin Country* won the MGM Award. That story too began and ended in Guernsey in the 1800s, and was based on a true story of a great-uncle, so no doubt that too owed much to Mrs Goudge's gift for storytelling. She was, however, 'no good with her pen', so although Elizabeth inherited her gift of storytelling from her mother, it was from her father that she inherited the talent and industry needed to write the stories down.

A third book, *Make-Believe*, published in 1949 as a story for children, also used material told to Elizabeth by her mother, and surely helped to compensate her for never being able to return to her native home.

The many similarities of the Collenette family to the fictional du Frocq one in *Island Magic*, make it interesting to compare the two.

When Elizabeth first went to stay with her grandparents they were living in a house in St Peter Port, but during the years when they were raising their family, they had lived in the parish of St Martin in a farmhouse known as 'Le Hêchet'. This house was surrounded by fields where the children could play freely, and nearby was a windmill belonging to a member of the same family of Ozannes as Marie-Louise—this too was a favourite place for the Collenette children to play.

When writing *Island Magic* Elizabeth moved her fictional family to another farmhouse that she said had always fascinated her, and she gave it the name of 'Bon Repos'. This house she described also as being surrounded by fields and near to a windmill.

To compare the real with the fictional family we need first to meet the members of the Collenette family.

Elizabeth's grandfather, Adolphus, had grown up in St Peter Port,

†† Although it was Elizabeth's first novel, it was not her first published book. *The Fairies' Baby and Other Stories* was published in 1919, but it was not successful.

living in the area called 'La Plaiderie'. This was conveniently close to the old hospital (now the police station) as his father, Dr Benjamin Collenette, was a member of The Royal College of Surgeons and was one of the best-known doctors on the island. Adolphus had four sisters and two younger brothers. Adolphus had hoped to follow his father into the medical profession, but soon after he started his training he was found to be diabetic. In those days, before insulin was available, this could only be controlled by keeping to a strict diet. Although he was to live to be over eighty, the diabetes affected his eyesight and caused him to go blind in his old age.

With the medical profession closed to him, Adolphus decided to use his medical knowledge by becoming a chemist, and until he was sixty he had a chemist's shop in the Commercial Arcade, near the marketplace. In those days a chemist provided help to people with minor ailments and injuries who could not afford a doctor.

He appears to have had many side-interests, which perhaps accounts for Elizabeth's hints that he was not considered a very successful businessman. His real love was for science and he was well known in the field of agricultural chemistry. With tomato growing one of the island's main industries at that time, he made an important contribution in that field.

Another of his interests was meteorology, and by the time Elizabeth went to Guernsey he was also well known for providing a daily weather forecast, displayed in a glass case outside the library. With island people more dependent on the weather than most, he was highly regarded for this work on the island. Instruments in his garden had to be read twice daily to gain the necessary information, and his family who got roped in to help called it 'doing the Obs.'

As for many men of his generation, his scientific work altered his religious outlook, and for most of his adult life he professed to be agnostic, but did not object to his family attending church. One wonders how Adolphus felt about his daughter Ida marrying an

THE OLD HOSPITAL IN ST PETER PORT, NOW A POLICE STATION
ST PETER PORT

Anglican clergyman of such distinction as the Reverend Goudge, but Elizabeth gives us no clue on that. She does tell, however, that on his first visit to the family before his marriage, her father was invited to preach in the Town Church of St Peter Port, when she said, 'the whole family trooped down to listen, afterwards expressing their approval of Ida's choice of husband'.

From Elizabeth's writing there's no doubt Adolphus was a kind and loving father who lived for his wife and children. Writing about him when she was seventy-four, Elizabeth said she still had the beautiful doll that he had bought for her in Paris on hearing of her birth.

Elizabeth remembered reading to him, when on a visit to them in England, after he went blind. She sadly recalled the despair he felt because his life's efforts would disappear at his death and go into nothingness. This caused her to re-examine her own beliefs, convincing her he was wrong.

Adolphus died on May 8th, 1922 at the age of 81. A long obituary appeared in the *Guernsey Times* recording his many scientific contributions to the island. It stated: 'his death removes a great personality from our midst—one possessed of a rare type of mind.'

Elizabeth acknowledged she based the character of André du Frocq on her grandfather, so the description of André she gave in *Island Magic* is likely to be the way Adolphus looked when she had first known him: 'small and thin, and bent with toil, his fair hair and beard already flecked with grey, his kind lightbrown eyes peering short-sightedly from behind glasses.' She gave the occupation of André as farmer and poet.

Elizabeth's grandmother, Marie-Louise, was also an interesting person and again she provided the basis for the character of André's wife, Rachell, with Elizabeth saying of the two portraits based on her grandparents, the one of her grandmother was probably the better one.

Marie-Louise had been one of six children born to William Ozanne and his wife Rosalie (Torode). At the time of the 1851 Census the family were living at 38 Rue Hauteville, St Peter Port. This house was later the home of the writer Victor Hugo (author of *Les Misérables*), having bought it from William Ozanne in 1856. The house has been kept as a memorial to Victor Hugo since his death in 1885. Elizabeth was taken to see the house and remembered how proud she felt to think that her grandmother showed Victor Hugo over the house on her eighteenth birthday.

In recent years a letter has come into the possession of the Priaulx Library, written by Marie-Louise to her younger sister Kate, telling her what their old house now looked like, and which parts had been altered. Giving news of the family in the letter, she ended by saying 'Dolph sends his love'.

Elizabeth admitted that she found her grandmother rather intimidating—very tall, dignified and beautiful, she was a strong character. I enjoyed the story about her umbrellas—she had three: one for wet weather, one for doubtful weather, and the third for use on the days when her husband could assure her it would not rain. How very useful to have an expert weather forecaster as a husband.

The description of Rachell in *Island Magic* was probably again true of Marie-Louise when she was young: 'a mass of dark hair piled in a high crown of plaits on top of her head.'

Adolphus and Marie-Louise had five children: Marie, Ida (later Mrs Goudge), Emily, Irene and William. Their oldest son had died when a baby. The fictional du Frocq family also consisted of five children: Michelle, Peronelle, Jacqueline, Colette and Colin. Three babies had been lost earlier.

Both mothers loved their children dearly, especially the sons. Sentiments expressed by Rachell on the subject of childbearing seem likely to have been real ones expressed by Marie-Louise which Ida passed on to Elizabeth: 'the producing of children ... Rachell considered perfectly detestable from first to last. She agreed with André that the human body was badly arranged. She loved her babies, but wished she could hatch them out of eggs.'

Another passage in *Island Magic* about Rachell rings so true that again I think it must have been something that Ida recalled about her own mother: 'After dinner Rachell went up to her bedroom. She always went away by herself for a little at this time and woe betide anyone who dared to disturb her. She guarded this little oasis of peace in her busy day fiercely and jealously. At other times of the day work and servants and children were claiming her, and at night she was her husband's. This was the only time when she belonged to herself alone.'

Another characteristic shared by the two women was their 'seeing'. Elizabeth said that this streak of extra-sensory perception ran in her family, but was only inherited by her mother and youngest aunt, and very little by herself. In *Island Magic* we witness how this manifested itself in Rachell's experience: 'At times Rachell had what the Scotch call "the two sights" and she had a "seeing" now. She saw Bon Repos as a little ark set in a waste of waters, surrounded by unimaginable dangers, a great darkness around and above it, hideous little waves licking its sides and fog wreathing around it. She knew quite certainly that her home, the cradle of her joys, was threatened … Then, not far from Bon Repos, she thought she saw through the fog the spars of a wreck, and from the wreck came a little boat with only one man in it … The light struck the man's face and she saw it clearly, a rugged ugly face, hard and self-contained, with a great scar across one cheek and an untidy thicket of grey beard emphasising the look of wildness in the eyes.'

It isn't long in the story before Rachell's 'seeing' becomes reality with a shipwreck and the saving of the man she has 'seen' who is to save the fortunes of the family at Bon Repos.

It's quite fascinating to follow the comparisons between the

Collenette children and their fictional counterparts. Marie Collenette was the clever one of the family. She later attended 'The Ladies' College at Cheltenham' and was eventually headmistress of a girls' school in England. The oldest du Frocq girl, Michelle, was depicted as studious, with a love of poetry, especially that of Keats and Shakespeare, and a great dreamer like her father.

Next came Ida Collenette, vivacious, with a gift of repartee, a lover of cycling and fencing and all outdoor pursuits. In writing the description of Peronelle in *Island Magic* Elizabeth was surely giving a childhood picture of her mother. '[T]hin, small, vital, with fair, curly hair that sprayed round her face as though each separate curl had a vivid life of its own. Her tawny eyes and pale pointed little face were the animated sparkling mirrors of every emotion that possessed her. Courageous, quick-tempered, generous, truthful, intolerant and passionately loving, she was a perfect whirlpool of emotion.'

Before going on to the next child, another passage from *Island Magic* about Peronelle conveys such a life-like picture of Ida as a child that it's worth looking at: 'It was Monday, and she was clothed in her dark blue school frock, a garment which she had long ago outgrown, but which even in its best days had not been designed to encourage grace in the female form. Her hair had been confined with such fierce determination in its Monday plait that it stuck out from her little head at an acute angle. Her long greeny-black stockings, from which her skimpy skirt withdrew in horror, were a marvellous example of the darner's art. Yet Peronelle, who all her life was to rise gaily above every misfortune, entirely transcended these disadvantages. Not even darned stockings and shrunken dresses could quench her magic.'

There are many other interesting stories about Peronelle in *Island Magic*, which can't all be included but which show Elizabeth was writing first-hand accounts given by her mother. There is, however, just one more that occurs twice and must be included. Rachell has been telling Ranulph (the shipwrecked stranger) some of the island's fairy legends, when he makes an odd remark about Peronelle: 'She has a larger share of fairy bewitchment than the rest, she should Marry Well.'

Emily, the blue-eyed daughter, who loved pretty clothes, was the aunt who, in spite of not being a good sea traveller, was the one who most often took Elizabeth to Guernsey. Like her fictional counterpart, Jacqueline, she seems to have been the most delicate one of the family and died in middle age.

The youngest girl in the Collenette family, Irene, was an extrovert. Elizabeth described her as 'the most determined woman I have ever known in my life'. As an adult she worked abroad as a nanny to royal families, when she was not averse to spanking her royal charges if necessary. She liked working in continental palaces, 'for they frequently had tiled floors, and it was easier to empty a jug of cold water over the head of a small boy in a rage than to spank him'. Although Colette du Frocq was only five years old when we read about her, the accounts of her escapades suggest she too was a very determined young lady. Her love for the irascible Grandpapa gave rise to this delightful aphorism: 'Extraordinary the affection which the worst of men can inspire in the breasts of the very best of the opposite sex.'

Elizabeth does not make much mention of her mother's only brother, William Collenette, when writing about the family in her autobiography, but this was probably because, for most of her childhood, William was working overseas, and was in Java when he sent his only daughter, Helene, to stay with the Goudge family when they lived at Ely, to start her education in England. They became very fond of her and she became like a sister to Elizabeth.

However, there is much in *Island Magic* about his counterpart, Colin du Frocq, that we are probably looking at a character very similar to the real boy in the Collenette family. Colin is described as: 'a nice small boy … and when clean, good to look upon. He was small for his eight years, exquisitely lithe and slender, dark-haired and brown-eyed, with a fair skin tanned by the sun to a warm golden brown … To add to his other attractions he had little pointed white teeth like a squirrel's, a very red tongue, whose tip was always to be seen peeping out at the side of his mouth when he was engaged in thought, small ears with the faintest suggestion of a fawn in their shape, and a dimple.' He was inseparable from his dog called Maximilian (which was also the name Elizabeth gave to the dog acquired from a pet shop in Wells).

An episode told about Colin may give another clue about William when he grew up. Colin has a stolen day out with his fishermen friends, which it was said 'he would recapture years later when he became a wanderer on the face of the earth'.

Another piece, allegedly about Colin, seems to me could only have been given by a sister, remembering a brother: 'so generous, yet such a shocking little liar, so courageous and yet so shameless'; and again: 'Colin had not at this period of his life, nor at any other, the smallest objection to telling lies. He liked things to be pleasant and agreeable all round, and he had found from painful experience that the giving of truthful answers to direct questions bearing on his recent whereabouts and behaviour invariably led to unpleasantness. Therefore in conversation he aimed always at giving pleasure rather than accurate information, and was throughout his life universally beloved.'

Peronelle, though loving her brother, could always see through his 'tales' more than the rest of the family. Was Ida the same? Whether Elizabeth based the character of Grandpapa in *Island Magic* on what she had heard from the family about Dr Benjamin Collenette is not clear, although I suspect there could have been a similarity between the two, as Elizabeth gives hints that the Collenette family, like the du Frocqs, were never very well off, and she said that in the early days of the marriage her grandmother had to help out by starting a little dame's school in their home. Grandpapa in *Island Magic* was certainly a tyrant and a sore trial to his son and daughter-in-law, as this account illustrates: 'Grandpapa, in a voluminous many-caped coat and with his beaver on the side of his head, stalked in. They rose and found him a chair, but he did not subside into it till he had stamped about the room examining it in minute detail. He ran his finger along the dresser shelf to see if it were dusty, he compared the clock with his own watch, he looked at the egg chart that hung on a hook by the fireplace, he picked up some diseased tomatoes out of a basket and looked at them, and he fixed his eye glass in his eye and stared for some minutes in complete silence at a damp stain on the wall. This behaviour he called "seeing to things at Bon Repos".'

What we do know regarding the great-grandparents is that Dr Collenette's wife, Martha's maiden name had been du Frocq, so Elizabeth had a ready-made name for her fictional family. The name of Adolphus's youngest brother was Ralph, again maybe a clue to giving the name Ranulph to the long-lost brother who was saved in the shipwreck.

There is no record of Marie-Louise visiting Ida in England, but they corresponded until her death in 1919. Elizabeth said that her mother inherited her grandmother's strong character but disguised the same iron determination with a velvet glove. Elizabeth inherited her tallness and dignity from her grandmother but her gentleness came from her beloved grandfather.

Guernsey was still unspoilt when Elizabeth stayed there, and the steamer arriving from England remained the island's main link with the world, just as it had been during her mother's childhood.

I wanted to arrive in Guernsey by sea, as Elizabeth had done, though the steamer service had long been replaced by a swifter service on the catamarans, and frequent air services have long ago abolished the isolation of the island from the rest of the world.

Although faster, the journey by sea can still be rough at times, and watching parents with young, restless children made me appreciate how plucky the 'Guernsey aunts' had been to undertake those journeys with the young Elizabeth.

The speed of the catamaran made it impossible for me to pick out the landmarks which indicated to Elizabeth how close they were to landing, and the old Albert Pier where Elizabeth's grandparents met them with a horse and cab, although still to be seen, is no longer the main landing pier. Today's passengers disembark at St Julian's Pier, where they are met by a fleet of yellow taxi cabs.‡ But the view of St Peter Port, with its tall houses, and steep narrow streets with cobbled surfaces, would still be very recognisable to Elizabeth today. Although the Channel Islands' connection with France was severed as long ago as 1548, the French influence is still apparent, with many of the street and house names in French.

The island is divided into ten parishes, each of which is run by an elected council known as 'The Douzaine', and they are responsible for the day-to-day running of the parish. During my visit I stayed in the parish of St Martin where, as we have already seen, the Collenette family lived in Le Hêchet, close to the Ozanne windmill.

There had been a considerable increase in the number of vehicles on the roads since my previous visit thirty years earlier, and I decided to make use of the network of mini-buses which provide a frequent service to all parts of the island. Although the speed limit everywhere is 30 m.p.h., the narrow roads do not make for relaxed driving, and often the mini-buses have to mount the kerb when passing. I found the drivers and local people so friendly and helpful it provided a good way to see the island.

There are many old farms to be seen all over the island—some

‡ In 2020 ferries dock at White Rock Pier and the taxis are no longer all yellow.

have old Norman archways with what is known as 'a marriage stone' set in over the doorway showing the date when a couple started life there together. It was probably one of these that Elizabeth remembered when she described the entrance to 'Bon Repos' in *Island Magic*: 'It was built of grey granite, with small diamond-paned windows and an arched doorway with the date 1560 on the central stone of the arch. Let into the wall above the door was a stone of much later date, bearing the inscription in French, "Harbour and good rest to those who enter here, courage to those who go forth. Let those who go and those who stay forget not God".'

I had corresponded with staff at the Priaulx Library in St Peter Port before my visit to Guernsey, as the library contains many old books and documents relating to the history of the island. One of interest was a ten-yearly Census form for the late 1800s, on which the Collenette family was listed as living in St Martin at 'Le Hêchet' farmhouse, though on the previous one the name of the house was given as 'Ruette Braye Lodge'. I found that the house has now been extended and is a hotel called 'The Braye Lodge'.

I spoke to people who had known St Martin all their lives, but they weren't able to help me locate which house Elizabeth had in mind for 'Bon Repos'. In *Island Magic* she had described its living room as 'a large raftered room, whitewashed, with a red tiled floor. The huge chimney had carved upon it the du Frocq arms, an ermine with the motto "Plutôt la morte que la souille".'

Later, when I contacted the island's archivist, Dr Darryl Ogier, to see if his records could help locate the building Elizabeth had in mind, he suggested she may have taken several characteristics of Guernsey domestic architecture to create the impression of a typical farmhouse of that time.

The 'Ozanne' windmill was fortunately easier to locate. Its sails have now disappeared and the machinery has been taken out to provide living accommodation, but it is still surrounded by fields as

THE BRAYE LODGE, FORMERLY LE HECHET FARMHOUSE—HOME OF THE
COLLENETTE FAMILY LATE 1880S
THE TOWN CHURCH IN ST PETER PORT

55

in the days when the Collenette children played there. The base of the windmill is now used as a workshop and studio for a talented jewellery designer, and it is her children who now ride their bikes and play around it.‡‡

Papers about the history of the mill are held at the Priaulx Library. The mill was built in 1825 by a James Ozanne, who had won a dispute with the Privy Council giving him and his fellow millers to do what they wished with their mills. The mill later became the property of William Ozanne, the father of Marie-Louise.

In 1885 it became the property of Joseph Ozanne, and it was struck by lightning in 1893 when one vane was lost. The opposite one was then removed and it was worked for twelve years with only two sails. It continued to be run by various members of the Ozanne family until it was sold in 1958 to Mr Fred Best, who lived at Sunnyside, the nearest property to Le Hêchet, on the Ruette Braye. His son dismantled the inside of the mill to make a delightful house for his daughter and family.

With their long connections with the parish of St Martin it is likely that members of both the du Frocq and Ozanne families attended the parish church, and also that Elizabeth would visit it during her visits to the island. A very unusual prehistoric statue known as 'La Gran'mère du Chimquière' stands outside the church gate and is thought to be a fertility emblem. The 13th-century church probably stands on another ancient holy site, so when the two broken pieces of the statue were found it was decided to play safe and place it outside the gate. It is the custom of couples marrying at the church to place offerings on top of her head.

A pleasant part of my visit was to explore the lovely bays and beaches which Elizabeth knew and loved in her childhood. They are still relatively unspoilt, and the twenty-seven beaches provide such

‡‡ In 2020 the jewellery designer is still there, but her children have grown up.

a variety of scenery—cliffs, coves, large stretches of sand—that there must be something for all tastes. Elizabeth said her favourite was 'Saints Bay'. At Rocquaine Bay, an old Martello tower, a relic from the Napoleonic War, has been adapted to house an excellent shipwreck museum.§ Although it was not there when Elizabeth knew the bay, the realistic reconstructions of some of the shipwrecks off the island, like those she wrote about, make interesting viewing.

The market in St Peter Port is still very colourful, though I didn't see the conger eel which Elizabeth wrote made a particular island delicacy, conger soup. Neither is it possible to hear the local patois spoken there. I was told that there are still older people speaking it who deplore its disappearance. They blame it on the large-scale evacuation of the younger people during the German occupation of the island in the Second World War. The islanders who stayed had a very hard time, and even after fifty years like to tell visitors about that awful time. Elizabeth's mother was very passionate about the English 'abandoning the island to the Germans', declaring, 'I will hate England until I die'.

You are never far away from the sea, and one of the things that Elizabeth remembered were the seagulls that fascinated her as she watched them, 'soaring, dipping, swerving, diving backwards and forwards, up and down, round and round'. She repeatedly used seagulls in her books, so that association is one today's visitors can share.

Many of the Guernsey family names used by Elizabeth are still to be found there today—the du Putrons, the Falliots, and Gossilins, as well as the Patourels and Ozannes. Many of the places Elizabeth knew can also be found—Castle Cornet, one of the landmarks she looked for on her approach to the island, now houses several museums. Victor Hugo's house, which belongs to the City of Paris,

§ Fort Grey Shipwreck Museum

can be seen furnished just as he left it, and a statue to Victor Hugo made from Guernsey granite stands overlooking the sea in the peaceful Candie Gardens.

Although the population of Guernsey has probably doubled since Elizabeth stayed there, and the tourist industry now makes a large contribution to its economy, there is still much beauty and enjoyment to be found there. This in part is due to the care that is taken to preserve the best for residents and visitors alike. The laws of the island are strictly enforced regarding litter and disorderly behaviour, which ensures a pleasant environment. Still known as 'donkeys' because of their allegedly stubborn nature, I found the local people very friendly and ready to pass the time of day or help with directions. Rachell's description of her island home still holds true: 'There's so much magic packed into so small a space. With the sea flung round us and holding us so tightly we are all thrown into each other's arms—souls and seasons and birds and flowers, and running water. People understand unity who live on an island. And peace.'

Maybe above all that is what Elizabeth retained from her childhood visits to the island.

GREEN DOLPHIN STREET—THE AMERICAN EDITION OF GREEN DOLPHIN COUNTRY. THE WRAPPER LOOKS VERY MUCH 'SET ON GUERNSEY' UNLIKE THE FIRST EDITION ENGLISH VERSION SHOWN RIGHT.

FIRMARY LANE, ELY. BACK WAY TO WHERE THE GOUDGES LIVED, PAST
HAUNTED BUILDING.

GROWING UP

ELY 1911–1923

The cathedral had nothing diaphanous about it but a great brooding presence that could at times be terrifying, so much so that at that time there were many people living in Ely who had never dared go inside it.

The first big change in Elizabeth's life came in 1911, when her father was offered a canonry at Ely Cathedral, combined with the principalship of the theological college.

The move took them from a small city set in a hollow, to another city built on a hill in the open Fen country.

Elizabeth later described it as 'the home of all homes'. Their tall house was at the summit of the hill, and she remembered looking over the vast stretch of the Fens. From the room that was first her schoolroom and later her bedroom, she could watch the sun coming up over the horizon, painting a huge skyscape of clouds: lilac, saffron, crimson and rose. It was this that led her to a love of Ruskin's writing with its description of skyscapes.

The cathedral soon took her captive. Known locally as 'the ship of the fens', Elizabeth thought of it more as a lighthouse so that when winter gales roared, or thunderstorms in summer darkened the sky, the tall tower was like a giant's arm held up to protect the city.

The move to Ely also brought sadness. With the new house and its upkeep proving expensive, the hard decision had to be taken that Nanny's services were no longer necessary. She was to return to their lives later, but the present separation plunged Elizabeth 'into total desolation'. It certainly didn't make the task of the new governess, engaged to prepare her for boarding school, an easy one.

Elizabeth's love of literature began during these Ely years. Her reading was prescribed by her father—under his guidance she progressed from the Andrew Lang fairy tales to the Waverley novels, Dickens, Thackeray, Trollope, the Brontës, and Jane Austen, who was to remain the inspiration of her own work later.

The Grassendale School in Hampshire was chosen by Elizabeth's parents as a suitable boarding school.† It may have been one known as suitable for children of the clergy as Elizabeth remembered 'they went daily for a tramp down the hill, the sea wind in our faces, to the parish church for matins'.

In her autobiography, Elizabeth described the school as an anachronism, as it did not appear to prepare its scholars for any future profession, but with the benefit of hindsight it is possible to argue that it may have been the right one for her future as a writer. It continued to build on her love of literature, which was to be the bedrock of her writing. This was due to the English mistress, Miss Bartlett, who taught her to love poetry, above all the poetry of Shakespeare. The school also encouraged a love of music that was to give her a lifetime of enjoyment—she played the violin in the school orchestra and learnt the piano. Miss Lumby, the headmistress, also seems to have had a lasting influence on Elizabeth during these school years spent during the First World War when telegrams would arrive, telling of the deaths of fathers and brothers of the pupils.

Elizabeth's love of the Hampshire coast and countryside, that she was to use as background to some of her most popular books, was kindled during these years. We have the first clue of her latent

† The borders of the county have since changed, and Southbourne, the location of the school, and its surrounding coastline is no longer in Hampshire.

FRONT OF HOUSE OCCUPIED BY THE GOUDGES SHOWING ELIZABETH'S
BEDROOM (USED IN THE FIRST EDITION OF *WEG*)
ELY CATHEDRAL C 1920

talent when one of her school reports made the suggestion that her gift of writing should be encouraged.

Travelling home to Ely for the holidays must have been quite difficult in those war years. Her father would meet her at Waterloo and they would then catch another train for Ely from Liverpool Street station. One Christmas holiday, before they continued on to Ely, her father took her on her first theatre visit to the Court Theatre for a matinee performance of *Twelfth Night*. That was such a supreme experience for Elizabeth that she became stage-struck and from then on, her scribbling efforts included plays as well as stories.

The war ended in 1918, as did Elizabeth's schooling, and the problem of what she was to do to earn a living had to be considered. Parents of that era realised that unless their daughters had exceptional beauty and charm, the pre-war expectation of marriage was no longer viable. The slaughter of the war had left few young men alive and the few who came home had been so exhausted that many had succumbed to the influenza that devastated Europe.

Elizabeth was obsessed by the thought of suffering, which led her to think she would like to be a nurse until the family doctor put a stop to the idea when diagnosing a heart complaint. As she liked making things, it was suggested that a training in handicrafts might be suitable, with the possibility of later teaching them to crippled children.

This idea was taken up. A friend of her father, Professor de Burgh, was vice-chancellor of Reading College where such a course was available, and she had cousins living in Reading who she could live with during term time.

After the war there was a great interest in handicrafts, and Elizabeth seems to have done them all during the course—metalwork, leather work, basket making, spinning, weaving, tapestry, embroidery and designing for textiles. As they were not allowed to use any patterns they had not designed, she also joined the art classes. Elizabeth said she was never as happy as when in the greenhouse where she studied flowers to use in designs later and, although she could paint flowers passably well, she could draw nothing else. She remembered how Professor Seaby, the head of the art school, stopped in front of one of her drawings and commented 'the worst drawing of the lot, but the best evocation of the atmosphere of a fairytale'. He wrote to her years later after reading one of her books, saying 'now you will be happy'.

The two-year course passed swiftly, and looking back on it Elizabeth said that learning to observe things in minute detail was excellent training for a writer, and was one that she could recommend to other writers.

Back home in Ely, she turned the old schoolroom into a studio, where for a short time she taught some of the handicrafts she had learnt.

Although there is no mention in her autobiography of any writing while she lived at Ely, she was certainly observing and absorbing much which was later used in her books. This is shown by the details she used thirty-seven years after leaving Ely, when writing *The Dean's Watch*, with the story revolving round the life of the cathedral, which she knew so well.

Visiting Ely to try to discover the influence growing up in the shadow of the great cathedral during the early part of the century must have had on Elizabeth, I was to find, nearly eighty years later, many changes, but also much that would still be familiar to her.

For someone who I knew loved mountains, I had always found it strange that she claimed Ely to be the dearest of her homes. The surrounding countryside of the Fens must be the flattest part of the country. However, now having seen it, it becomes clearer why this place retained such a strong hold on her affections. Even today, it seems a place remote from the modern world, and this would have been more so at the time she lived there when transport and communication were more limited.

Even on a short visit you immediately get a feeling of freedom, with the open skies and far horizons. The surrounding flat countryside emphasises the slight hill on which Ely stands and the spiritual impact of the huge cathedral, dominating the whole area, remains long after your visit.

This combination of strength, spirituality, and a degree of aloofness from the world around, seems to epitomise Elizabeth's own innate character—by her own admittance she was never at ease with everyday social life, taking after her father who once stated 'he would have been happy in the monastic life'.

The house where the Goudge family lived is very close to the south side of the cathedral. The main part is now the Deanery, but their former kitchen is used now as the Chapter Office. Above it is the study used by Canon Goudge which Elizabeth said, 'he loved with all his heart' because he was working on a level with the old Norman arches that formed part of the infirmary chapel of the former Benedictine monastery. It is now used as his study by the present Dean.

A short walk from the former kitchen door down Firmary Lane, leads to the south porch of the cathedral. On a gloomy March day as I walked there, it was easy to understand the suspense that Elizabeth felt on winter nights as she walked it alone, with 'a haunted house on the right and another to the left'. The one on the left was known as the Painted Chamber. During monastic times, it had been used by female visitors to the sick monks in the infirmary, but when alterations were carried out, the skeleton of a monk who had been walled up was discovered.

With her vivid imagination, Elizabeth would have wondered how that must have felt. The only reference I found to her was in a book in the cathedral bookshop called *Haunted Ely*, which includes her account of her ghostly experiences in Ely, including the one about the faceless monk who often came to her room. I was interested to

ENTRANCE TO WHERE WALLED-UP SKELETON WAS FOUND
(USED IN THE FIRST EDITION OF *WEG*)

EMBROIDERED BANNER OF ETHELDREDA
(MODERN PHOTOGRAPH)

read that even recently the ghost had been seen by other residents. The book gave a possible explanation for these appearances, and Elizabeth, with her interest in historical research, may also have known it. Apparently, the monks used to attend the infirmary once a month for a blood-letting session, thought to help subdue their sexual desires—the amount of three pints a month is quoted. The story suggests that an unfortunate monk was tempted, by one of the visiting females, to sin before reaching the infirmary. He was discovered and given that awful punishment as a warning to others. The Painted Chamber now houses scholars from The King's School, but as the ghost only appears to the ladies, they need not worry.

Although Ely was home for twelve years, Elizabeth was away at boarding school and college also during that time, so possibly the time spent home during the holidays made those years extra memorable. Another reason for remembering them so happily is because the drier climate resulted in an improvement in Mrs Goudge's health, always a great concern to Elizabeth. It meant these adolescent years were reasonably carefree and happy, and she seems to have enjoyed more social activities than at any time in her life. There was ice-skating on the frozen Fens, where she 'floundered along, clinging to the back of a chair'. There were water picnics and boat outings in the summer. She rode the local lanes known as droves on a pony borrowed from the milkman. Older now, she could accompany her father on walks in the surrounding countryside, where he would show her the rare butterflies and plants native to the area.

The love of music gained at school must have been augmented in the holidays by the music in the cathedral, and her love of beauty by the glorious cathedral building and the special festivals of the church's year. One of these was the festival of St Etheldreda on October 17th, still held today. An embroidered banner of this saint is displayed and carried in procession on special feast days. Elizabeth always loved the autumn and said 'she hoped John Donne was right in thinking it would always be autumn in heaven'.

The cathedral would have been decorated for this festival with all the lovely autumn flowers giving out their special pungent smell, which years later would remind her of Ely. I like to think she would enjoy a recording made by the present choir called *Evensong for St Etheldreda*.††

Although the tortoise stoves that heated the building rather inadequately in her day can still be seen, they are now gas fired and seemed very efficient on the cold day I was there.

In 1986 a £4 million appeal was launched for the complete restoration of the cathedral. Much careful work had already been carried out and hopefully the task will be completed during the Millennium year.* The lovely painted ceiling above the nave has been cleaned and restored to all its glory. After two years' closure the Lady chapel is once more open, providing a spacious area lit by large plain-glass windows. During the years Elizabeth lived at Ely it was used as the parish church.

Although the theological college has been closed for some time, ordination services are still held in the cathedral. The college building is now part of The King's School. I found an amusing story about former theological students in a book by Pamela Blackman.‡ 'As they went from the college to the well known hotel, "The Lamb" at the top of the town, they had to pass a certain lamp-post which they would describe as "a light to shine upon the road that leads me to the lamb".'

†† Released by Herald in 1997
* Now complete—service of rededication attended by the Prince of Wales
‡ Sylvia Gower meant the Ely historian Pamela Blakeman. In her book, *The Book of Ely* (1990) there is a footnote on p.129: 'The lamppost said by the students of the Theological College in the words of the hymn to be "A light to shine upon the road That leads us to the Lamb." .'

With her love of animals, I like to think it would please Elizabeth to know that an annual service is held in the cathedral to which a varied assortment of animals are brought for blessing. This is just one aspect of the way in which the cathedral tries to cater for a wide range of interests in the community. All very different to the cathedral that Elizabeth described in *The Dean's Watch* when Isaac, the watchmaker, like many other residents of the town, was terrified of it and never dared to go inside.

The association and remembrance of people with places is one we all experience and this was true for Elizabeth and Ely. There was her much-loved cousin Helene, who first came to stay with them there in her school holidays; her Aunt Emily brought her Guernsey grandfather there for his last visit and Elizabeth remembered reading to him as he had become blind.

It was here, she confides in her autobiography, that she was in love for the first time. Although 'it ended in tears', we can perhaps venture a guess as to who this might have referred to. Was it a student at her father's college, an actor from the local operatic society, or perhaps a fellow student at Reading?

On April 24th, 1921, Elizabeth celebrated her twenty-first birthday. A traditional gift at that time for such an occasion was a gold watch, so it is possible one was bought for her at a watchmaker in the town. In an old directory for 1850, five watchmakers were listed, so one may still have survived. Could it have been one Elizabeth recalled forty years later when writing *The Dean's Watch*? Even today, some of the shop fronts lend themselves to picturing Isaac's shop or the tiny one of Miss Bertha Throstle where the Dean bought Bella's umbrella.

Although, because of the cathedral, Ely has city status, it remains a pleasant market town, with a variety of individual shops. With new amenities added to those Elizabeth enjoyed, it appears a good place in which to grow up.

Electricity reached Ely around 1915. Before that all the streets and domestic lighting would have been supplied by gas and candles. It was probably some time before all households were connected, and it may never have been introduced into the Goudge household.

The telephone had arrived in 1905, and I like to think that Mrs Goudge, with her active mind, would have insisted on having that social amenity installed.

Many of the streets and buildings of Ely could still be recognised by Elizabeth, although some have different uses. The Bishop's Palace has not been the residence of the bishop since 1940 and at present is a Sue Ryder Home. Oliver Cromwell's House, formerly St Mary's Vicarage, is now an attractive tourist office.‡‡

Elizabeth berated herself that, with the First World War starting at the same time as her departure for boarding school, the latter had had more impact on her. I think she can be excused because in a book I bought about Ely memories covering a hundred years from 1891, I did not find any contributor mentioning that war.

Ely suffered little or no war damage, not even in the Second World War. I found a reference to Zeppelins passing low over Ely and I believe the tower of the cathedral was a good navigational guide to pilots on both sides.

If Ely escaped lightly in wartime, it had experienced tragedy in the previous century when it was devastated by a cholera epidemic in March and April of 1832, probably caused by a lack of good water supplies. Eventually, this resulted in mains water being available to all by 1852. However, there was still a great deal of poverty and sickness in the early 1900s due to poor living standards. Elizabeth, inheriting the compassionate nature of her parents, was aware of this, partly through the ministrations of her father who acted as an

‡‡ In 2020 the Bishop's Palace has become the sixth form centre of The King's School (now called King's Ely), while Oliver Cromwell's House is a museum as well as a tourist office.

orderly at the hospital in World War 1, but also because when he visited the poorer houses, he would sometimes take her with him. She remembered her distress at what she saw and wrote of similar conditions in the fictional 'St Swithin's Lane'.

All the places and characters she drew upon forty years later, show how vivid her memories were of the years lived at Ely. She remembered the willow trees that provided material for the osier and basket-making trade; the Fen villages and sunsets; the warm woollen clothes worn to keep out the intense cold in winter—flannel petticoats, serge bloomers, gaiters, muffs and mittens. She recalled how at first the local people seemed dour and difficult, but she came to recognise this sprang from wrestling a living in the harsh conditions, and to appreciate their courage and toughness.

She found it a paradise for the botanically minded as well as the historically minded, of which she was both. She knew the history of Hereward the Wake and the early monks of Ely, and used this knowledge in *The Dean's Watch*. She found the herons, tall and meditative, had for her the same effect as the windmills and church towers, breaking the flatness of the Fens.

In a preface to *Three Cities of Bells*, this is what Elizabeth had to say about Ely and *The Dean's Watch*: 'No writer can ever truly be said to like a book he or she has made because the book written down falls so tragically short of the book in the mind before it was written, but there is always one we care for more than another and in the (unlikely) event of our being remembered after our death we would like it to be this book. *The Dean's Watch* is for me this special book. Its cathedral city is even less like Ely than Torminster is like Wells, and the cathedral reminds readers more of Lincoln than Ely, yet this for me is Ely, the most beloved of all my homes and the cathedral that all through my growing years possessed me with its splendour … It dominated everything, always. Wherever you went in the Fen country you had only to look up and see it there, riding the sky like a great ship. Yet whether riding the sky, or towering up above the scared yet exultant ants of human creatures it sucked into its dark porches it was always, in all weathers, whether its mood was terrible or beautiful, a symbol of eternal life.'

Elizabeth explained that in the many years between seeing the characters and writing about them, Adam (the Dean) had become possessed of much of her father's character. So too after so many elapsing years, other people, places and events have changed, and to visit Ely trying to identify it with the book, will probably lead to confusion. To visit it to experience some of the timeless beauty of the cathedral and surrounding countryside that made Ely such a special place for Elizabeth, is certainly rewarding.

THE APPROACH TO THE CATHEDRAL FROM ELIZABETH'S HOUSE

THE FIRST EDITION OF *THE DEAN'S WATCH*

TOM QUAD AND CHRIST CHURCH

OXFORD HIGH STREET 1920s

BECOMING A WRITER PART 1

OXFORD 1923–1939

Essentially Oxford never changes. Old shops and dwelling houses may be swept away and when they are lovely one may grieve to see them go, but the essential Oxford is what it always was, a power house of the knowledge for which men are always searching.

Like most of us, Elizabeth did not welcome change. Looking back on our lives we often acknowledge that the changes forced on us led to wider horizons and new opportunities.

Had Elizabeth's quiet halcyon life at Ely continued, the stimulation that a new environment was to give to her writing might not have allowed her talent to develop so successfully.

After the ending of the First World War, the theological college at Ely reopened. Canon Goudge stayed to see it through that difficult period, but, when a new post to teach theology at King's College London was offered, he felt ready for the change. He retained his canonry position at Ely, returning there at the weekends. By now he was regarded as one of the foremost theologians of the time, and in 1923 was offered one of the Church of England's highest posts—that of Regius Professor of Divinity at Oxford.

Always a humble man, he did not want this honour and agonised as to where his duty lay. He was also concerned about the effect such a move might have on his wife's health, as a house in Tom Quad at Christ Church college went with the position. The river mists from the nearby River Thames might not be as healthy as the drier air at Ely.

Pressure to accept the post came from all sides, and some astute person realised that if Mrs Goudge could be persuaded of the benefits, she might use her influence with her husband. Unlike her husband and daughter, Mrs Goudge was a very socially minded lady, so when she understood that the position ranked with that of a bishop and a presentation at court was a possibility, she appears to have supported the move.

Later, Elizabeth said she thought her father knew of these ploys, but kept quiet. His socialist views ensured he would not be interested in any such advantages the post might offer.

Finally, the decision was made to accept the offer, and in the spring of 1923, the family and three maids moved to Oxford. Elizabeth certainly kept in touch with friends at Ely for many years, but there is no mention of her ever returning there.

Sadly, very soon after the move, Mrs Goudge suffered what Elizabeth described as 'a despairing breakdown'. After reading the description of the large, gloomy house, with its high population of mice and a smaller one of rats, it is not surprising. Even the garden did nothing to cheer her spirits—she thought it a draughty, stuffy town garden, only redeemed by an Acacia tree in the north-west corner, which, when in bloom, was one of the sights of Oxford, and popular with painters.

Back in the city where he had spent his student days, Canon Goudge was instantly at home, so Elizabeth and her mother did their best to hide their feelings of dismay about the house. The contrast between the simple life at Ely and that of a busy university city could not have been greater. The summer was a whirl of social events, which would have suited Mrs Goudge immensely had she been well, but an earlier operation for sinus trouble meant she could not tolerate noise. The constant pealing of bells and chiming of clocks, as well as the activities of the students, caused her unbearable distress. The open windows during the hot, airless days of that first summer, made her family realise a solution to her problems must be found.

The nearest place near to the sea that could be reached by train was New Milton in Hampshire, and a swift visit there resulted in their renting a bungalow at nearby Barton-on-Sea for the rest of the summer. Elizabeth saw her mother safely installed with her favourite maid before returning to Oxford to act as housekeeper and hostess for her father for the rest of term time.

This established the pattern for their lives for the rest of the years at Oxford. For £500 they purchased the bungalow at Barton where Elizabeth and her father were also able to join her mother during the Easter and summer vacations, enjoying the simpler life that gave them. Mrs Goudge was able to spend the worst of the winter months back at Oxford, where closed windows and warm fires made it acceptable to her.

This new situation at Oxford was very daunting to Elizabeth. She was expected to return numerous social calls, and her shyness and the stutter she had acquired at school made her very nervous. Her hands would tremble as she rang the bell, fervently hoping the people were out.

Although Oxford was never her favourite home, she eventually found many compensations for the dreary house and her social obligations. Being young and active, she was able to explore the adjacent countryside, delighting in the kingfishers in Christ Church Meadow and bluebells in Bagley Wood. She was able to escape from the hustle and bustle of the busy city to the cloisters of Magdalen and New College gardens. After a while Elizabeth admitted enjoying some of the new experiences which living in Oxford gave her.

Their home in Tom Quad was right in the hub of college activities, with Tom Tower to the right, the cathedral and Deanery on the other sides of the quad. Their front windows looked over the green lawns surrounding the well-known Mercury pool and fountain.

Having to accompany her father to social functions meant Elizabeth met some of the well-known characters who lived in Oxford in the 1920s and 1930s, such as Dr Spooner, the warden of New College, whose amusing habit of transposing initial consonants gave rise to the term 'spoonerisms'. One example she gave of these was, when speaking to a lazy student, he told him, 'Sir, you have hissed all my mystery lectures and tasted the whole worm'. She also knew the colourful, but absent-minded Monsignor Ronald Knox, the son of an Anglican bishop; he was converted to Catholicism, and became the Catholic chaplain at Oxford from 1923–1939.

Elizabeth's love of the theatre was revived by visits to the Oxford Playhouse where she saw plays by Ibsen, Shaw and Galsworthy amongst others. Occasionally she got to a London matinee, and remembered seeing John Gielgud in *Hamlet*.

Although Elizabeth was still earning a small pittance teaching handicrafts, she decided to try her hand at writing plays, thinking they would be shorter and easier than novels. Three of these were eventually produced for charity performances in London, but a publisher to whom she had sent them, advised her to change to writing novels. She took his advice and, as we have seen, her first novel, *Island Magic*, was published by Duckworth. This led to being asked to write short stories for *The Strand Magazine* as well as two more successful novels.

Her father, she said, persevered in reading a chapter a day of her first three novels, but found them very hard going. Her fourth novel, *Towers in the Mist*, seems to have pleased him more, probably as he wanted to see what use she had made of the books he had borrowed for her from the Christ Church library.

It must have been difficult for Elizabeth to have her scholarly father as her critic. She tells of a remark her father once made about her writing: 'You have such a wonderful gift,' he said, but before her head could swell, he continued, 'you can make a little knowledge go a long way.' Had he lived to read the rest of her books (*Towers in the Mist* was his last), I think he would have realised just what a wonderful gift she did have, for although her books were based on places she knew well, she was able to transform them into magical places.

It may well have been at her father's suggestion that she chose the subject of Elizabethan Oxford for her novel, wanting to please him. Her first novel was dedicated to her mother and now the fourth one was dedicated to her father. She chose an appropriate quotation from the writing of Philip Sidney, who had been a student at Christ Church, to accompany the dedication: 'Here now have you, most dear, and most worthy to be most dear Sir, this idle work of mine; which, I fear, like the spider's web, will be thought fitter to be swept away than worn to any other purpose. But you desired me to do it, and your desire to my heart is an absolute commandment.'

Elizabeth said that it was because she did not much like the Oxford of her day that she decided to find out about an earlier time in the city. As Christ Church had been founded (as Cardinal College) by Cardinal Wolsey in 1525, and re-founded by Henry VIII in 1546, the early Elizabethan age seemed a rewarding age to choose for her research. Writing an introduction to *Three Cities of Bells*, in the part relating to Oxford, she wrote that to start with the modern town seemed to be 'a solid, immovable curtain blocking out the past', and she despaired of ever continuing her book until, suddenly, 'the curtain went up and the old city … with its cobbled streets and tumbled roofs' came vividly into her mind's eye.

The story begins when Elizabeth I is Queen and Oxford was becoming a place of importance to both merchants and the students flocking there. She brought several historical personages into the story, including Walter Raleigh and Philip Sidney, admitting she brought him there a few months early for the purpose of her story.

The Leigh family, on whom the story centres, she made to live in the same house in Christ Church as the one in which she was living.

The whole novel is captivating in the manner it depicts how people had lived in that exciting but dangerous time when the burning of the religious martyrs was still fresh in their minds. The head of the family is Canon Leigh, who relies on his oldest daughter Joyeuce to organise the rest of his large family since his wife has recently died. The household also consists of Faithful, a dirty, ragged but clever boy who the family have taken under their wing, a terrifying old aunt, and a collection of animals who join the family in their daily prayers.

We share the hopes and dreams of the family over a momentous year in the life of the city, culminating with the visit of the Queen— we are given a glimpse of the history of Oxford from the time when the early settlers had noticed a patch of dry earth between the two rivers, and decided it was a secure place to stay.

Everyone reading the book will find passages of special interest to them. One of my favourites is when the Leigh family are attending the Sunday service in the cathedral and Joyeuce finds solace from her personal problems in the beauty of the building: 'The Saxon pillars of the choir, massive and of colossal strength ... and the perpendicular clerestory that rose above them, and carried the eye up to the fine and graceful pendant roof, seemed like the arches of the years that carry a man's soul from the heavy darkness of the physical earth to the airy regions of heaven ... Ancient glass, that told the story of Saint Frideswide's life, filled the windows and the sun shone through it to pattern with all the colours of the rainbow pillars and arches and the tombs of the dead that paved the floor.'

We are given a glimpse of the different modes of worship that Canon Leigh would have experienced during his lifetime.

'The great days of Cathedral worship, those days when the music of the Mass sounded like angels singing, and the incense drifted

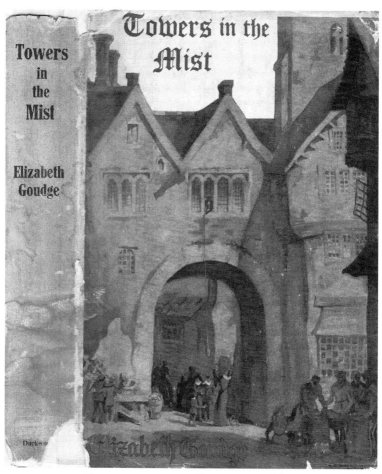

THE FIRST EDITION OF *TOWERS IN THE MIST*

in a fragrant cloud through the pillared aisles, had gone forever, but in this service of the reformed religion there was both dignity and beauty. The choir sang the psalms of David with simplicity … and the prayer that Cranmer had written, repeated by Canon Leigh in his deep and beautiful voice, had a haunting beauty that smote hard upon each heart. "O God, the protector of all who trust in thee, without whom nothing is strong, nothing is holy; increase and multiply upon us thy mercy, that, thou being our ruler and guide, we may so pass through things temporal, that we finally lose not the things eternal".'

Only ten years before, Archbishop Cranmer, after being imprisoned by Queen Mary in the Tower of London, had been brought to the Bocardo Prison in Oxford, together with his fellow bishops, Ridley and Latimer. He had seen them taken to be burnt to death outside the North gate, before he was taken to the cloisters and subjected there to degrading treatment, before he too was burnt at the stake.

All of this is recalled by Canon Leigh: 'In no part of the College did Canon Leigh feel so aware of the passing and re-passing of ghosts as he did in these cloisters, for here, at the heart of Wolsey's College, the old Priory that had succeeded in Frideswide's Nunnery still seemed to have its stronghold. To the north was the monks' Cathedral Church, to the east the Deanery that had once been the Prior's house, and at right angles to it the monks' refectory that was now the library, and in the centre of the enclosed square of grey stones, the remains of the monks' washing place showing through the green grass.'

I wonder whether Canon Goudge, as he read his daughter's book, recognised the similarities between himself and the fictional Canon Leigh?

So many historically based incidents that appear in the book show how carefully Elizabeth did her research. There is an account of a fight that erupted between the 'Town and Gown' elements in the city which were quelled by Dean Godwin on horseback—a typical occurrence in those times. The book looks in on Walter Rayleigh locked in the Bocardo Prison and wondering whether there would ever come an age when all the world would be known, and thanking God that he lived 'when it was still possible to sail out into the blue, and build a new empire for his country'.

As well as being a fine romantic story, and historically interesting, *Towers in the Mist* points to the emerging philosophical side of her work, as when Faithful feels the family needs comfort to cope with Christmas coming so soon after the death of Giles, the oldest son of the family: 'Faithful decided he had better read aloud to his adopted family, and fetched his beloved "Book of Martyrs". It had accompanied him through all the many changes and chances of his own life and he had always found it an unspeakable comfort. Not only was the example of the martyrs so uplifting but it was really impossible to think of one's own woes when absorbed in blood-curdling descriptions of other people being burnt alive. There is nothing like the troubles of other people to distract one's attention from one's own.'

The Leigh family were expected to vacate their house for the Queen's use during her stay in Oxford which caused many aggravations, especially to Aunt Susan, who refused to move. The last three chapters deal with great drama about the Queen's visit, doing credit to Elizabeth's former aspirations to be a playwright. The visit in August 1566 lasted for several days and was during the early part of her reign. It was claimed that the Queen loved learning and could debate in Greek or Latin with the best students of the day. Usually the students went home in the summer to help with the harvest, but this year they had to stay until after the visit ended.

Queen Elizabeth was to visit the city again twenty-six years later, and the story relates that on saying farewell to the place that had welcomed her so magnificently, her eyes filled with tears, as she had a presentiment how, by that time, she would be a weary old woman, worn out by years of unceasing work and anxiety, and doubted if the shouts of 'Viva Regina' would then be as full of love from her subjects as they had been on this one.

Writing in her autobiography about the years spent at Oxford, Elizabeth compared the students then with those she remembered, and concluded that the present ones seemed more concerned about injustice and exploitation than their grandparents at the same age, but she thought their compassionate anger, without discipline to curb it, could prove destructive. She ended by saying, 'Perhaps what the world needs is more compassion, more and more of it not for human beings only, but for every single living creature whose small span of life and enjoyment can be shattered by lack of it'.

Although we can understand why Oxford wasn't Elizabeth's favourite home, we can still be grateful for the part it played in those early days of her writing career.

Like Queen Elizabeth, I too visited Oxford in August, when the noise of students is exchanged for that of tourists from all corners of the world. Even so, Elizabeth's remark, 'essentially Oxford never changes', seemed in many respects to be true. Although there are now car parks on the perimeter of the city with a shuttle bus to bring in passengers, the traffic still flows unceasingly along the main streets. Fortunately the colleges still retain their green spaces within a stone's throw of the busy areas.

Oxford has been in the forefront of the car industry, ever since William Morris (later Lord Nuffield) began to make motorcycles there and went on to produce the Morris Oxford. The car industry has brought great prosperity to Oxford: the endowment of Nuffield College as well as other educational bodies.

The other William Morris, British craftsman, poet and painter, also has associations with Oxford. He studied there in the 1850s,

CHRIST CHURCH CATHEDRAL FROM THE CLOISTERS

and one example of his work—a stained-glass window, can be seen in Christ Church Cathedral. Elizabeth was a keen admirer of his work when she was a student at the Reading School of Art.

I wanted to begin my 'footsteps journey' in Oxford by visiting Christ Church and locating the house where the Goudge family had once lived. I made my way from Carfax, at the hub of the city, down St Aldate's, recollecting this is where Elizabeth said their charlady had lived with her numerous cats. I quickly found myself at the main entrance to Tom Quad, but I was not allowed in that entrance, but directed to one further down the street where visitors are charged for admission to the college.

As soon as you turn off the street you are in Memorial Gardens. It was laid out in 1925 so Elizabeth would have seen the inscription from *The Pilgrim's Progress*, 'My sword I give to him that shall succeed me in my pilgrimage'.

Before turning into the college, right ahead of me lay the inviting Christ Church Meadow which stretches right down to the River Thames. It was given by a Lady Montacute to ensure the maintenance of her Chantry in the Lady chapel at the Priory of St Frideswide, which once stood on the site of the college. The rights to the meadow are carefully guarded, cattle still graze there, and wild flowers bloom in their season. I wasn't able to discover if this still includes the fritillaries in the spring for which it was once famous. On a hot summer's day, it was a pleasant start to my visit to see families enjoying the green space so close to the bustling city, and to know that the environmentalists of 1965 had won their battle to prevent a road being put through the fields.

The buildings of the college stood out clear against the summer sky, and it seemed a good thing to me that, in spite of all the changes in the outside world, this site, ever since the building of St Frideswide's Priory in the 8th century, has remained dedicated to worship and learning.

I passed through the cloister where Archbishop Laud had stood before making my way into Tom Quad. The quadrangle was designed by Cardinal Wolsey, but only three sides were built before his fall from favour. The fourth side was completed in the 1660s. The Tom Tower above the main gateway was designed by Sir Christopher Wren in 1681. It houses a six-ton bell which originally came from Osney Abbey, which was abandoned after Henry VIII re-founded the college.

Having heard this bell striking midday as I turned off St Aldate's, I began to understand Mrs Goudge's problem when coming to live in Tom Quad, especially after reading that at 9.05 p.m. each evening the clock strikes 101 times, marking the number of the original students plus a scholarship student.† Hopefully today, double glazing makes the noise more acceptable for present residents.

Using Elizabeth's description of their house, I easily located the building they once occupied. I learnt later it is still the domain of the present Professor of Divinity, although much modernised since the Goudges' years there.

Going under the archway towards Peckwater Quad, nothing remained to be seen of the Acacia tree in the north-west corner of the garden, but behind me was the library from which the books were borrowed that helped Elizabeth with her research for *Towers in the Mist*. My guidebook stated that there are 120,000 books and old manuscripts kept at the library.

I retraced my way back to the cathedral. It dates from the 12th century, and is one of the smallest in England. Built on the site of St Frideswide's convent which was burnt down in 1002, the present building was begun in the 12th century by the Prior of the Augustinian Order, and has been added to over the years. It has some

† 9.05 p.m. corresponds with 9.00 p.m. Oxford time, rather than Greenwich Mean Time. It still strikes 101 times in 2020.

beautiful stained glass, including a 14th-century window depicting St Frideswide. Church music has been important in the cathedral ever since Cardinal Wolsey appointed the composer John Taverner as its first organist. A helpful cleric on duty in the cathedral when I visited, suggested looking in the chapel where there are memorial tablets to some former canons. Not surprisingly (knowing what an unassuming man he had always been), we did not find one to Canon Goudge. Elizabeth said that her father's social conscience had not always made him popular with the college authorities, especially when he raised awkward questions about slum properties owned by the church.

I saw as much of the rest of Oxford as time permitted, some of it from the top of the bus where a commentary is given as it goes round the main places of interest. It has of course expanded since the Elizabethan age featured in *Towers in the Mist*, but due to the age of most of the colleges, has not changed as much as other places in that time. I was interested to see examples of the gargoyles being carved to replace the old ones of buildings. The local stone used on many of the older buildings is very friable, and constant work is needed to maintain it. They are still being made as caricatures of local college people, just as the old ones were.

The Oxford Playhouse is still producing plays, though whether it is still at the same venue that Elizabeth knew I couldn't discover.††

On the outskirts of Oxford, where Faithful Croker stayed with the gypsy family before setting off to try his fortunes in the city, Shotover is now a country park.

I learnt that at Magdalen College, the choir still welcomes in the festivities for May Day from the tower at 6 a.m., followed by bell

†† The Oxford Playhouse was built in 1934, so today's building is the same one Elizabeth would have visited, although it has since been completely refurbished.

ringing and Morris dancing as they did in the Elizabethan times and as described in *Towers in the Mist*.

Reading the book before my visit to Oxford helped me picture it, as Elizabeth had done so successfully, without modern-day distractions obliterating the glorious heritage it offers to today's visitors.

INSIDE CHRIST CHURCH CATHEDRAL

THE GOUDGE MEMORIAL CROSS, NEW MILTON (USED IN FIRST EDITION OF *WEG*)
(SEE PAGE 115 FOR HOW THE GRAVE LOOKS NOW)

BECOMING A WRITER PART 2

BARTON AND THE HAMPSHIRE BOOKS

I owe more than I can say to Barton. Here I really discovered the Keyhaven saltmarshes that had caught hold of me in my schooldays, and it was from Barton that I first went to stay with Mrs Adams at the house I have called Damerosehay.

If Oxford provided the stimulation for Elizabeth to become a writer, then Barton was the right environment to make it possible. She said in her autobiography, 'I owe more than I can say to Barton, my hobby of writing got more and more hold on me'.

When they first went to Barton, she was young, well and active. She loved walking, so it was mostly on foot that she resumed exploring the area she had known during her schooldays. Even though her father was a keen cyclist there is no mention of Elizabeth ever owning a bicycle. Possibly her mother's cycling accident made her parents too apprehensive to encourage it. The family never owned a car, and Elizabeth never learnt to drive.

She recalled that the area from Poole to the Solent was still unspoilt by development in the 1930s, and she must have found walking there delightful in the spring and summer months, after leaving the strictures of Oxford behind her.

Their small bungalow, purchased for £500, was set in a country lane running parallel to the coast, and was surrounded by fields separating them from the fast-growing town of New Milton where they arrived by train at the start of their visits to Barton. The lane of bungalows would probably, like those built in other coastal places during that period, have been mainly intended for holiday occupation. The nearest church was St Mary Magdalene, two miles away at New Milton, where Canon Goudge assisted the Reverend Hutchinson at services when he was at Barton. They were also not far away from the lovely Christchurch Priory, famed for its music.

Their dog, 'Brownie', came with them to Barton, and in the evenings Elizabeth remembered walking with him the short distance to the coastal path, 'to watch the last lights fade from sea and sky'. He had been given to them by Marie, and the description Elizabeth gives of him makes it seem likely that Pooh Bah, and The Bastard, the dogs in *The Bird in the Tree*, were based on Marie's Chow, Swankie, and her son, Brownie. Brownie died at Barton and was to be the last dog Elizabeth had until 1951, although the way dogs always featured in her books shows how fond she was of them.

Elizabeth said she wrote her first novel, *Island Magic*, in the corner of her mother's bedroom at Barton. Mrs Goudge's poor health meant she often had to rest. It's possible to imagine Elizabeth encouraging her mother to talk about her memories of Guernsey to take her mind off her ailments, while she continued with the book.

Until the 1930s, travel had not been part of Elizabeth's lifestyle— her income from teaching handicrafts had not been sufficient. After the success of *Island Magic*, and short stories published in *The Strand Magazine*, all this changed and she wrote, 'Barton was the point of departure for what for me was high adventure'.

Either Nanny would come from Bath, or the aunts from Guernsey, to stay with her mother at Barton, while she went on walking holidays with a friend to the Lake District, and saw the high hills she had dreamt about in Westmorland and Cumberland. They spent blissful days, finding remote farmhouses to stay where a packet of sandwiches would be provided as they went on their way the next day. Elizabeth would take her paintbox with her and attempt to record the beautiful scenery. Needless to say she was never satisfied with her efforts, but the pictures in her mind would later be translated to word pictures in her writing.

More walking holidays followed to Scotland and the Hebrides, to the mountains of North Wales and Norway. Knowing how cruelly Elizabeth was to be afflicted, comparatively early in her life, with arthritis, it is good to reflect on those happy holiday experiences, which all provided material for her writing.

As her success continued she went on a wonderful cruise with her father and Aunt Marie to visit the classical sites around the Mediterranean, seeing the Acropolis, Troy, Crete, Corsica, Syracuse and Constantinople (now Istanbul). With typical humility, Elizabeth felt her cousin Helene was more deserving than herself to see these wonderful places.

The advice given to her by her agents Nancy Pearn and David Higham to write short stories for a living while she built up her reputation as a writer, was responsible for the collections of stories later published by Gerald Duckworth. Originally commissioned by *The Strand Magazine*, the first collection in 1937, under the title *A Pedlar's Pack*, deservedly reached a wider readership. Another collection of earlier stories appeared in 1941 with the title *The Golden Skylark*, and in 1943 more earlier stories under the title of *The Ikon on the Wall*.

Later, when Elizabeth was at the peak of her fame in 1952, the three collections, together with two new stories and a foreword by Elizabeth, were published under the title of *White Wings*. This book continued to be reprinted up until 1975.

Everyone reading the stories will have their favourites—there is something to please all tastes, from historical stories like 'The King's Servant' about Sir Thomas More, to ones about literary characters as in 'The Golden Skylark' about the poet Shelley, and there are biblical stories 'By the Waters of Babylon' and 'Son of David'.

Perhaps one of the best loved is 'Dogs of Peking'—the story of Wang, king of the lion dogs at the Imperial Palace at Peking, and the impudent Mee-Too, who saves the emperor's life. Stories in the later collections reflected the events of the time, such as 'The Ikon on the Wall', written when Russia and Finland were in the foreground of war news.

Twenty-three stories make up the *White Wings* collection, and each and every one has character studies as outstanding as those in her novels, and shows clearly the research she did for each one.

In the foreword to the collection Elizabeth sets out in her modest and honest way, the way she saw the joys and drawbacks of the writing profession. She said she had found short stories much harder to write than novels. I find myself almost regretting that her success with novels meant she stopped writing short stories. If I were ever asked which of her books I would choose to take on a desert island I think it might have to be *White Wings*, as to me it includes all the qualities that came out in her later writing.

One of the walking holidays in Scotland and Skye gave Elizabeth the idea for her third novel, *The Middle Window*. Published in 1935, Elizabeth later said it was her least favourite book, although she didn't give her reasons for that. I believe it was because it used reincarnation as the main theme, which she tells us her father dismissed as 'utter nonsense' when she discussed the theory with him. Writing forty years later, she said at that stage she did not think her father could be wrong, adding, 'I think now he may have been wrong'.

It was written at a stage in her life when she was groping for answers that her 'inherited beliefs' didn't give, which makes it interesting—not a clergyman in sight! The story tells of a dual romance, one set in the 1930s, and the other in the 1740s. In the first period we meet Judy Cameron, who after seeing a picture in a window in London of a remote Scottish Glen and then finding an advertisement for a similar place to rent, persuades her wealthy parents and doting fiancé that her happiness depends on going there. The property belongs to an impecunious, but idealistic laird, Ian Macdonald, who is trying to improve the life of his tenants.

With the family settled in the house, and with hints of a mystery lurking about the place, we are transported back during a thunderstorm to the late 1740s, when after the defeat at Culloden the Laird Ronald Macdonald is led by a signal from his wife from 'the middle window' to think it is safe to return. Unwittingly she has led him into a trap and the lurking English soldiers capture and kill him. His grieving wife orders the window to be boarded up and lives the rest of her long, lonely life with only an old faithful servant, Angus, for company. Having already been introduced to a cantankerous present-day Angus, we realise he must be a link with the past.

Back in the 1930s, Judy and Ian become more and more aware of an affinity drawing them together. The highlight of their romance is their day's outing together to Skye, and the terrifying thing Judy experiences on the moors there.

Elizabeth had been to Skye and had experienced a very frightening and unexplained sound on the moors which she put into this story. She had paused on her climb to look at the mysterious range of hills known as 'The Cuillin', completely alone and no one in sight, when the silence was shattered by a loud rapping noise, that sent her scurrying back to the safety of the Ardvasar Hotel, which in the story she had Ian tell Judy is 'the friendliest hotel in all Scotland'.

Elizabeth wove past events to influence and bring the modern romance to a satisfying end. Her love and knowledge of poetry enabled her to give extra poignancy to her books by quoting apt pieces as prologues or epilogues. In the epilogue to *The Middle*

Window, 'The Finding', she quoted Samuel Butler to give it an appropriate ending:

> 'Yet for the great bitterness of this grief,
> We three, you and he and I,
> May pass into the hearts of like true comrades hereafter,
> In whom we may reap anew and yet comfort them,
> As they too pass out, out, out into the night.
> So guide them and guard them Heaven and fare them well.'

It was quite a dramatic story and was later written as a play, but does not appear to have been performed. An idea perhaps for a future production, even, with the present vogue, a musical.

While the books known as 'The Eliot Trilogy' are always associated with Hampshire, only the first part of the first of those books, *The Bird in the Tree*, was written while Elizabeth was at Barton. However, as the setting for the books was certainly drawn from the years she lived there, it would seem the most appropriate time to look at them.

Life at Barton brought its share of troubles as well as pleasure. Mrs Goudge's health continued to be a cause of concern, and during their time there she had two operations on her back, as well as a severe illness. When Canon Goudge also had to go into hospital, the constant worry affected Elizabeth's health, and led to a nervous breakdown and other health problems needing treatment in hospital.

During this time, friends mentioned a peaceful hotel in Keyhaven, called Harewood House. It was owned and run by a Mrs Adams, who, after the death of her husband, had decided that rather than move, she would offer accommodation in her beautiful home near the peaceful marshes of Keyhaven. She only took guests who were recommended as being likely to appreciate the peace it offered.

It provided the perfect place for Elizabeth to recuperate, and as soon as she got back to her writing she decided to make it the setting for a fictional family called 'The Eliots'. Searching for a suitable name for the house, she remembered hearing the romantic name, 'Damerosehay' which was the name of a field separating Keyhaven from Lymington. The name derived from one given by refugees from the French Revolution who had settled in Lymington.

She then found fictional names to conceal the identities of other local places she would use in the book. Milton on Sea was changed to Fairhaven, and divided into 'Little Village' and 'Big Village'.† Elizabeth remembered hearing during her school excursions about the great storm at Keyhaven which had caused a ship carrying grain to be wrecked on its shores. Her imagination went to work on that event and the result was *The Bird in the Tree*.

But sadly, soon after starting on the book, Elizabeth and her mother had to cope with a sorrowful event in their lives. The family had arrived to spend the Easter holiday of 1939 at Barton. Over the festival, Canon Goudge, now 72, had assisted at various services—in Bournemouth, Bristol, and New Milton—but the following week he had a severe fall. Within two weeks he died in hospital—it was April 24th, Elizabeth's thirty-ninth birthday. Each subsequent birthday she must have been reminded of that sad day.

The funeral was held at New Milton church with a guard of honour formed by ex-theological students he had taught at Wells. His ashes were later interred in the cemetery of the same church, where later those of his wife and daughter would be placed. A memorial service was held at the same time at Christ Church, Oxford, where tributes were paid to this well-respected and renowned theologian.

After the first phase of shock and grief, Mrs Goudge and Elizabeth coped the best they could with the turmoil of packing up the home at Oxford, and all the burdens that follow a bereavement.

† Sylvia Gower possibly meant Barton-on-Sea.

Nanny, now retired, came from her home in Bath to give invaluable help. They felt fortunate that, unlike many clergy families, they still had their home at Barton to fall back on.

It was nevertheless a very difficult and dismal time, and Mrs Goudge suddenly decided that they needed a holiday. She answered an advertisement for a cottage to rent in the village of Marldon, near Paignton in Devon. Plans were quickly made to take it for the summer, but fate was to play its hand, and with the outbreak of war, when an offer was received to buy the bungalow at Barton, the decision was taken to stay and make a new life in the place they both already loved—Devon.

Their changed financial circumstances meant it was vital for Elizabeth to get back to her writing, so in their rented home which they called 'The Ark' she again took out the unfinished manuscript of *The Bird in the Tree*. So much had happened since she had written the first instalment, and the book's setting now seemed so remote, that she found it a struggle to go on. In desperation she prayed that she might dream the rest of the story, and she claimed that was exactly what happened. Writers are often advised to keep a notebook by their bed, to put down ideas that might come in the night—so maybe that is what Elizabeth did.

Knowing this story, other readers of the book may, like me, wonder where the break came in the writing. There seem to me to be two possible places—the first when Lucilla and David first see Damerosehay. While David goes to explore the garden, Lucilla, who has got up early, falls asleep and has a wonderful dream of being in heaven. A few weeks before she had sat at the deathbed of her favourite son Maurice, just as Elizabeth had recently sat with her father. Had that experience been Elizabeth's also, so that it was possible to write it into the story?

The second place I think possible is further on when David Eliot is gripped by the nightmare of the imminence of war that he fears will destroy all the creativity which is a vital part of his being. After the loss of a loved one, our minds go over all that made that person so special to us. Canon Goudge had held very clear-cut views about war, which Elizabeth would remember, and this passage might be her recalling them, as she wrote about David's gloomy forebodings.

Delightful as Elizabeth's early novels were, I feel it was only after her father's death that the philosophy that was to make her writing so special, became increasingly evident. It has been observed that we often take on the characteristics of someone close to us after they have gone—Elizabeth had always loved her father dearly, but for most of her life his brilliance had rather kept her in awe of him, though in the last year they had become closer.

She certainly inherited her father's aptitude for hard work as the output of her work in the following years proves, in spite of the difficult war years, caring for her mother, and her own increasingly poor health. I think it can be seen how she seems to have acquired many of his other characteristics—the same compassionate outlook, social awareness, humility and, dare it be said, his saintliness. Much would of course have been absorbed during her years of living with him, but I believe they became her own values more noticeably after his death.

After the huge popularity of *The Bird in the Tree*, Elizabeth eventually wrote two more books about the Eliot family which were spaced over a period of thirteen years. The second book, *The Herb of Grace*, was published by Hodder and Stoughton in 1948,†† and the third one, *The Heart of the Family*, in 1953. In each book the saga of the Eliot family continued but reflected the time gap that had occurred since the last one and the way in which national happenings had altered the family's fortunes. There were no TV soap operas to be kept up with, and the fortunes of the Eliots gave readers a similar

†† *The Herb of Grace* was published in the USA as *Pilgrim's Inn*.

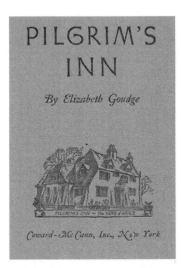

The title page of *Pilgrim's Inn*, 1948, the American edition of *The Herb of Grace*

Harewood House (Damerosehay) (used in the first edition of *WEG*)

sense of knowing them as real people. New characters joined the original ones to keep the interest flowing in the family.

The owner of Damerosehay, Lucilla Eliot, plays a central role in all three books. Elizabeth said there was something of her mother in the make-up of Lucilla, but that is the only clue she gave to any resemblance to an actual person, though I think it is possible to detect some others for ourselves. Ellen, Lucilla's faithful maid, seems to have much in common with the Wells Nanny, while the unmarried daughter Margaret who is devoted to her mother (and much put upon), bears some resemblance to Elizabeth. Hilary, the balding bachelor clergyman, could be based on many of their clergy acquaintances, while David, the favourite grandson, brought up by Lucilla, sounds very much like the young Henry Goudge, who had also been devoted to his mother.

The theme of *The Bird in the Tree* can be summarised as duty and faithfulness, which may sound dull virtues to today's readers but at the time it was published reflected a current debatable topic coming soon after the marriage of the Duke of Windsor to Mrs Simpson. I found an interesting story from a magazine of the time, when a young couple wanting a divorce were advised by the judge to go away and read the book. Apparently they were so influenced by David and Nadine's decision to put their own desires aside so as not to hurt others, that they patched up their differences and stayed together.

The paper giving the story added, 'the author of the book was a spinster', which shows how some people were intrigued at the way Elizabeth was able to empathise with people outside her experience. Not only did she have a natural compassion and intuitive understanding for a wide range of problems, her upbringing in a clergy household would probably have meant that she heard a variety of personal problems being aired from an early age. Her retentive and imaginative mind responded with an awareness of the joys and tragedies in life, far more than most others.

When *The Herb of Grace* was published, the war was over but many couples were finding it hard to adjust to living together again and could relate to Nadine's struggle before recommitting herself to her marriage to George. Many other women like Jill, who had returned to the family as a nursemaid, were having to make new lives for themselves after the death of their husband. Other people were trying to search for new truths after the old values had been swept away by the war years. All these changes in society are reflected in the book by this perceptive writer.

Similarly, by the time *The Heart of the Family* appeared on the bookshelves, the awful tales of the concentration camps and war atrocities had filtered out to the public, so that the introduction of Sebastian, a former inmate of a concentration camp whose entire family had perished in the war, was again very relevant. Sebastian is secretary to David Eliot, now a famous actor living at Damerosehay with his wife and children, Lucilla and Margaret having moved to nearby Lavender Cottage.

Sebastian's sufferings and bitterness are taken on board by all the family, with Lucilla remembering that she had heard him play when he was a famous pianist in pre-war Europe. Sebastian's acceptance of his suffering before his death, shows how Elizabeth could take these and other adversities affecting her characters and apply Christian values in meeting them. It was this that so often brought solace to readers who had been through similar experiences.

As well as the Eliot Trilogy, Elizabeth used her memories of Hampshire to write a children's book, *The Valley of Song*. She said it was one of her favourites, perhaps because it was written 'Under the shadow of death' during her mother's last illness. Its setting is at Buckler's Hard, in the days of its fame as a centre for building sailing ships including Nelson's *Agamemnon*. It was not as popular as the other children's books, being too mystical for many, but worth reading before a visit to Buckler's Hard today.

THE FIRST EDITION OF THE OMNIBUS, *THE ELIOTS OF DAMEROSEHAY*

Knowing Elizabeth's love for Buckler's Hard, in 1950 friends there asked her to write a guide book to the little chapel that had just been converted there from one of the cottages. That guidebook can still be found in the chapel there today.‡

After her mother's death in May 1951, Elizabeth went to stay at Harewood House for the last time. She found it was beginning to look shabby, and also the garden overgrown, staff now being difficult to obtain. Quite soon after this Mrs Adams decided to sell the house, and for a while it was run as an ordinary hotel. This didn't prove successful and eventually it was left empty and became ruinous, until finally it was bulldozed to the ground with no trace left of the gracious house and garden.

Elizabeth heard the sad news from the former postmistress in the village, and later in her autobiography wrote: 'one of the things in my working life about which I am most thankful is that someone or something prompted me to write three books about an imaginary family living at Damerosehay, and that those three seem to be my readers' favourites. As long as the three books are read Damerosehay has not quite vanished from the world and I have not lived in vain.'

As I set out to follow in Elizabeth's footsteps in Barton and Hampshire, my first visit was to the church and cemetery of St Mary Magdalene in New Milton. Elizabeth had given the town the fictional name of Radford in her book, describing it as a new town with a spread of bungalows. The town has continued to grow since she wrote that, as the huge number of graves in the cemetery signified. In spite of my misgivings when approaching the cemetery from the newer end, I was able to find the Goudge Memorial Stone fairly easily, as it stands in the older part by a path leading to the church, surmounted by a large cross.

‡ Published as *The Chapel of the Blessed Virgin Mary, Buckler's Hard, Beaulieu*, 1958.

THE COTTAGES, BUCKLER'S HARD, THE RIVER TO THE LEFT

INSIDE THE CHAPEL OF THE BLESSED VIRGIN MARY, BUCKLER'S HARD

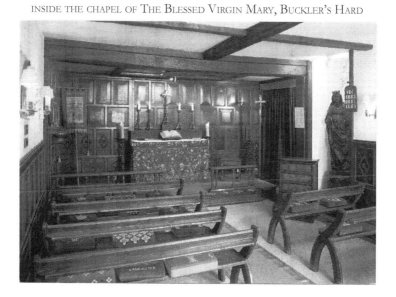

The first text, engraved in 1939, reads: 'He asked life of Thee, and Thou gavest him a long life: even for ever and ever.' Another text was added when Mrs Goudge's ashes were interred in 1951: 'God proved them, and proved them worthy for himself.'‡

Thirty years later, when a horizontal slab was placed on the grave, an inscription was added with the words: 'And their daughter, Elizabeth Goudge. Beloved Author 1900–1984.'

It was a strange and poignant experience, when on a bright, chilly March day, I stood looking at this memorial marking the end of the earthly journey of the family I was now so involved with. Would they regard my interest as impertinence and wish to be forgotten? Or, would they, as I hoped, understand my conviction that Elizabeth's writing can still help another generation to find new values in their lives?

I recalled an incident that Elizabeth recorded about a childhood memory—'the three of us were on the same hearthrug together, our arms about each other, and my mother was saying in a clear voice, "A threefold cord shall not be broken".' Elizabeth always said she owed much to being part of a loving family and this is reflected in her writing about the relationship between her characters.

Like most churches these days, St Mary Magdalene would normally have been closed between services, but a door was being repaired, and on explaining my interest I was able to look inside. The present church is on the site of a smaller one used until the 1920s, when the town's rapid growth necessitated its enlargement in 1928. A Lady chapel was added in 1958, and the present church is a light and spacious building.

I continued my journey to Barton Lane, where I found the fields that used to separate it from New Milton had long been built on.

‡ This part of the inscription is no longer on the grave. Possibly it was on the cross, which is missing in 2020.

Although most of the former houses have been pulled down and replaced or modernised, the lane still retained a rural feel as when the Goudges knew it.

Their bungalow, 'Innisfree', was one of the ones recently replaced, so it was not possible to know exactly where it stood, but seeing periwinkles growing by one entrance may have given a clue, knowing Elizabeth's love of that plant.

The former coastal path where Elizabeth walked with Brownie is also much developed, but when I continued my journey a little father along the coast to Keyhaven I found it was still relatively unspoilt and quiet, at least on the early spring day when I saw it. The lovely marshes fringed with seagrasses were still as Elizabeth had described, and the little harbour, now classed as a marina, was peaceful with the rigging tinkling in the breeze as the ships rocked on their moorings.

Looking across to Hurst Castle, the description Elizabeth gave is as apt today: 'an ominous mass lying crouched upon the water like an animal on guard.' The island on which the castle stands can be reached by a causeway of shingle at low tide, or by boat when covered.

Inland, peaceful, flat grazing meadows could still be seen. Inside the village pub, 'The Gun', close to the harbour, nautical mementoes suggest the figure of William Urry might appear round the corner any minute. Elizabeth changed the name of the pub to 'The Eel and Lobster', and lobster pots adorn the outside walls as they probably did when she knew it.

The postmistress who wrote to Elizabeth about the end of Harewood House still lives locally and treasures the letter she received in reply. She is able to confirm that the story of the grain ship wrecked on the shore which Elizabeth used, did actually take place, though Obadiah and the blue bird brought to safety in its brass cage were Elizabeth's embellishments to the story.

Another person living in the area has interesting recollections about Elizabeth and her family. She attended St Brandon's school for clergymen's daughters in Bristol around 1919, when she remembers being taught the Psalms and catechism by Marie Collenette (Aunt Marie). She remembers her as being small, dark and vivacious, and thinks she was later vice-principal at the school. Elizabeth mentions that she lived at Stroud in the Cotswolds, so that is quite likely. Another aunt, Emily Collenette, also taught at the school and died tragically when middle aged. Marie used to tell her pupils about the niece 'who wrote stories' and she once visited her aunt, when she was remembered as 'quiet, shy and very blonde'.

This same lady tended the Goudges' grave for many years until she became too frail. It seems that flowers still appear anonymously on the grave at times.

Another resident of Keyhaven who lives in one of the houses built on the former site of Harewood House in a small development known as Harewood Green, possesses a photograph of the former house given to her by the builder. The photograph shows a long, rambling building, walls covered with climbing plants, and set in spacious grounds framed by lovely old trees. A paperback edition of *The Bird in the Tree* shows a similar scene, so the artist for that may have been shown the same photograph to assist him.

Some of the trees shown were surely the old oaks that feature in the story, with at least one holly tree where the blackbird sang. I like to think there would have been a wild garden at Harewood House like the one in Damerosehay which was always a special place for all the Eliot family.

On my visit to Buckler's Hard after many years I was very relieved to still find it peaceful and beautiful as I had remembered it and as Elizabeth had described it in the Eliot books. The only change is a small visitors' centre which provides information and houses an exhibition of models of the ships that were once built and launched from the Hard. Although my visit was at an off-peak period, I felt confident that even at the height of the tourist season visitors must still be able to appreciate the essential peace it offers.§

The times Elizabeth used it in her books show how much she must have loved it there. In *The Bird in the Tree* David takes Hilary for a drive in his car, 'to the place that had once been the most important shipbuilding centre in England and was now only a short little street of eighteenth century cottages leading down to the quiet reaches of the river'. It is here in 'The Master-Builder's House' (now a small hotel) that over tea Hilary gave David his 'lecture' on the subject of faithfulness, which was to influence David's decision to part from Nadine.

I too had tea in that pleasant room with its beautiful engravings of sailing ships and looked out of the window as Hilary had done when reflecting, 'perhaps Portsmouth will be as derelict as this is—given over to the herons and the gulls, with only a grey donkey to walk about its streets'. Having just come from Portsmouth, I could only rather wryly observe that fifty years on, that fantasy of Hilary's hadn't come to pass, even though the bombing of the German Luftwaffe had done its best to make it so.

In *The Herb of Grace* George and his children stop at Buckler's Hard on their way to inspect the old inn on the river, which Lucilla has already decided would be the ideal place for them. They are all transfixed by the lovely place, with Tommy in his outspoken way saying, 'Only fools would live in London'.

Finally, in *The Heart of the Family* a stop is made again at the Hard on the way to visit George's family now living at 'The Herb of Grace'. This time the group included Sebastian, the war refugee.

§ The small visitors' centre has since expanded into a maritime museum, shipwright's workshop and numerous other attractions, but the village's website still describes it as a 'peaceful haven'.

His thoughts had been dwelling on the fires of Hamburg and for a moment he imagines he sees smoke drifting over this place too and comments 'it is a pity the rest is destroyed'. David's reply gives reassurance: 'only by time, not by violence.'

Another visit to the little chapel reminds us that it was a cobbler's shop in the shipbuilding heyday, but later was used as the village dame's school, before its transformation into the little chapel we see today. We ended our visit again reading from Elizabeth's guide: 'It is not possible that so lovely a way can lead to anything commonplace. He (the traveller) has a feeling that he is coming to something that will be part of him for the rest of his life. This is no longer an excursion, but a pilgrimage, he is not a tripper any longer but a pilgrim.'

Ever since the publication of the Eliot Trilogy readers have been drawn to visiting the places she wrote about in Hampshire for themselves. One place they haven't found is 'The Herb of Grace Inn': nothing like it exists on old maps of the area, so we have to assume it was a rarity in Elizabeth's writing—a purely fictional place.

To finish my footsteps journey for this period of Elizabeth's life presented a problem, for not even the most adventurous biographer (which I certainly do not claim to be) could hope to retrace all her walking holidays which provided material for her writing. I decided a visit to Skye would be an interesting choice to represent that pre-war period in her life.

In *The Middle Window* it was high summer when Ian and Judy set out for their day in Skye. The summer vacation, released from her duties at Oxford, would most likely have meant Elizabeth also visited at about the same time of year.

My visit had to be in early autumn, and because the recently opened Skye Bridge had resulted in making the small ferry crossing from Mallaig very infrequent, I had to opt for a more comfortable but less romantic way to reach Skye. The lovely scenery of lochs and hills along the road approaching Ardvasar, after the bridge crossing, compensated for the loss of romance, and as I reached the turning to the village that joined the road up from the ferry I was able to relate to that part of the experience described in *The Middle Window* where Judy and Ian had walked up from the ferry crossing: 'The clouds had blown away and the sun was shining down from a brilliant blue sky upon a rain-washed island where every leaf and blade of grass seemed sparkling … in front of them rose a wooded slope, the green trees in their ranks marching right down to the sea. Where Judy expected to see silver sand she saw instead grass of an almost savage green, with the blue water rippling in and out between the tussocks. The blue and green were pierced by grey ridges of rock where the gulls and cormorants were sitting solemnly, making a pattern of black and white against the brilliant colour. The sparkling clearness of it reminded Judy of a Chinese painting of an earthly paradise she had once seen and it was not until they … were walking along a winding road under the great trees, that the familiar smell of ferns and wet earth made her realise that this was still the British Isles … They turned to their left and followed the road until the trees thinned and vanished and they found themselves in a crofting township. White-washed houses stood in gardens protected by thick hedges of fuchsia and on their right was an old white-washed inn. "The Ardvasar Hotel," said Ian …

'On the left, between the road and sea, were fields of flowers. Yellow vetch, yellow daisies, tall grasses, pale lavender scabious and creamy meadow-sweet were swaying in the wind. To the right, behind the crofts, the moors were rolling to the skyline.'

It was a magical experience to walk along that road over sixty years later, to see and smell the same things. We found the hotel just as hospitable as they had done, and sat in the dining room kept cool by its three-foot walls. Instead of oatcakes our coffee was served with the most delicious shortbread. The air of complete contentment everywhere made me hope the little maid in the story was right when she said to Judy, 'They all come back, they don't seem to help themselves'. I could understand how, when a French journalist was interviewing Elizabeth in the 1960s and mentioned she had just visited Skye, she recorded how Elizabeth's eyes lit up as soon as she mentioned Skye.

If the years spent in Oxford and Barton are considered to be those when Elizabeth was 'becoming a writer', her apprenticeship was more than successfully completed, as they came to an end.

LEFT AND ABOVE: THE GOUDGE GRAVE AS IT IS NOW IN 2020.
(SEE PAGE 6 FOR DETAILS OF THE JUST GIVING PAGE TO INSTALL A NEW CROSS.)

THE FIRST EDITION OF *WHITE WINGS*

FOREWORD TO THE COLLECTION OF STORIES CALLED *WHITE WINGS*

THE ENTERTAINMENT OF STORY-TELLING

How wonderful it must be to write stories, say the friends of the story-teller, and there are both admiration and envy in their tone. As for the admiration, the story-teller knows he does not deserve it; he knows perhaps that he turned to woo the lady make-believe because he was too unpractical to manage a business, lacked the courage to become a doctor, was too weak of character to impose discipline on classes of unruly children; the admiring friends can do these things, but he, faced with the problem of earning a living, could do nothing but step backward into the past and recover its memories for their entertainment.

For story-tellers know what is the source of the misplaced admiration; they, as well as actors, clowns, and conjurers, are public entertainers, and from the dawn of the world the entertainers have been placed upon pedestals because they can amuse the world, make it lay aside its worries for a short hour as it watches players upon a lighted stage, or forget its pain as it holds a book in its hands and cries aloud like a child at night time, 'Tell me a story. Light the candle and tell me a story.'

And so crowds throng a stage door to watch a famous comedian pass through it, but the great doctor who has saved a hundred lives goes by unheeded; the yearly income of a successful dramatist will go into thousands when a scientist can barely earn a living; such a price are men willing to pay for a draught of the waters of Lethe and a tale told at bedtime to make them forget their fears of the dark.

There is no foundation for the admiration, the story-teller knows, but there may be for the envy. Is he to be envied? Sometimes he resents the envy of his friends. They seem to think the work of the story-teller is all so easy. He merely sits down, dips his pen in a bottle of ink, and inscribes upon paper the ideas that flow in a never-ceasing flood of brilliance through his fertile brain. He need not go out into the rain to earn his living, as they do, he sits comfortably at home by a roaring fire. He can choose his own time for working, abandoning all labour when he has a cold in the head and taking to it again when his sneezes subside. He is his own master and his own pupil, he need neither obey nor get himself obeyed. When he owes money to his dentist he has but to compose a story in his bath, and when they are after him for the rent a few flourishes of his pen will scatter them again … It is all so easy.

So say his friends, and sometimes, with that strange desire of human nature to be thought a martyr, he frets and fumes a little. What do they know of the bad times through which he passes and the problems and fears that hedge him about? Those days of ill-health or worry when both imagination and brain refuse to function; those days when troops of glowing images throng the imagination but the dulled brain can find no words with which to catch them; those other days when words stand all ready to attention like well-drilled soldiers but there is no vision to set them marching. And then the fears. Will the book be finished in time? Will the publisher accept it? If he does, will the critics tear it, this beloved child of the story-teller's mind and soul, into shreds and tatters? Above all, will readers be disappointed? And always present with the poor story-teller is the problem of adjustment. How can he live the life of imagination and the life of the world at one and the same time? If he breaks off in the middle of a particularly fine passage—or what he thinks is a particularly fine passage—to answer the call of the dinner-bell the fine passage will be ruined, but if he does not answer the call of the dinner-bell the cook will give notice. Then if he withdraws into a secret world of his own to write his story, as of necessity he must if it is to be well written, will he not become one of those monsters of selfishness who refuse to be bothered with other people's worries or to rejoice in other people's joys, who say, 'Go away,' when a knock comes at the door and, 'Can't you see I'm busy,' when a friendly face peers in at the window? … Thinking it all over the story-teller comes to the conclusion that he should be pitied, not envied. The perpetual harassment of his soul in this world and its everlasting damnation in the next seem all he has to look forward to … He wishes he was one of those men who wave a red flag in front of a steam roller or walk up and down at a railway station tapping train wheels with a hammer. Then and then only would his soul know peace and safety.

But then he thinks again. He remembers the joys of his profession too many and too various to be counted, but all of them rooted in the fact that he is an entertainer who entertains not only others but himself. It is from the entertainment of others that his chief joys spring; from that correspondence with readers who tell him that the thoughts of his mind have given them pleasure, strangers who do not know him and so can write those appreciative letters that more than make up for the candid criticisms of the friends who, knowing him only too well, are aware of a little inconsistency between thought and action; and from the happiness of the creator who knows that puppets of his own making are telling a tale of his own contriving to a listening audience; but the entertainment of himself is no mean joy either, for it is the joy of memory.

In no way can the past be recaptured more vividly than by writing about it; the pen seems like a key to a storehouse of treasures. If a writer sits down to write of childhood he is amazed at the multitude of memories of his own childhood that come running to greet him. Figures that had grown dim are once more clear to him; he looks into their eyes and hears them speak words that he thought he had forgotten. He basks again in the warmth of suns that were surely hotter in those days than they are now, and smells the scent of flowers whose petals faded and dropped twenty years ago. Birds sing their spring songs to him, even though as he writes it is midwinter, and soft little furry beasts, dead for years past, scamper in green fields that are now overlaid with bricks and mortar … For memory has a happy faculty of shedding a clear light over past joy and dimming the outlines of pain. We recapture the first so vividly that we clasp it to us like a child in our arms, while we hold the second only at arm's length … The entertainment of memory is one of the best entertainments this life can give us; well worth that rather bitter moment when the curtain drops and the lights fade out and we are back again in the drab present.

But the writer's material is not only his own past; the past of his family, of his country, of the whole world, is his to entertain himself in as he will; in remembering tales that others have told he can link his own memory to the memories of those others and recreate for himself kings and queens he never knew, cities and forests, battles and tournaments and ships he never saw. And as with personal memories, so with these; it is when we tell a tale about them, rearranging old facts into a new pattern, that they come alive and let us out into a country of enchantment where we are children again.

For no one is more childish than the story-teller, sitting by himself in a corner building towns and houses, making people to walk in their streets and tables and chairs to furnish them, dipping into his memory for just the right man to stand in that patch of sunlight and just the right bird-cage to hang in that window; between him and the three-year-old rummaging in his box of bricks for one that looks like a chimney there is surely no difference worth mentioning. Certainly he is to be envied by his readers, those wise and courageous ones, those teachers and doctors and men of science, for children are happy people and much entertained by their make-believe ... Though not to be set on a pedestal, for surely it is quite out of the question that maturity should admire childishness ... Yet, on second thoughts, readers should take thought before they mock, for when they sit down at twilight, open a book, and cry, 'Tell me a story,' are they not children too?

I imagine Elizabeth wrote this foreword for *White Wings* when it was first published in 1952 although it was reprinted again in 1952, 1966 and 1975.

Even in 1952, some of the things referred to such as men walking with a flag in front of steam rollers and cooks who gave notice if one was late for meals must have been rather obsolete, but add extra interest because of it.

To some, the foreword may seem rather verbose, but for others, especially other writers, the humorous allusions to their trials and joys will make it very enjoyable.

PROVIDENCE COTTAGE
(AS IT APPEARED IN THE FIRST EDITION OF *WEG*)
PROVIDENCE COTTAGE TODAY

SUDDEN FAME

DEVON 1939–1951

The valley below was even wider and deeper than I had realised the night before and it seemed to hold every beauty that a pastoral Devon valley knows, woods and farms and orchards, green slopes where sheep were grazing, fields of black and white cows, and where there were fields of tilled earth it was the crimson of the earth of South Devon and looked like a field of flowers.

Devon? Why Devon? Nanny and I were dumbfounded. She and I had never been there, and my mother only for a short while.'

This is how Elizabeth described the decision to go to Devon in the summer of 1939. Intending to rent the wooden bungalow for a month's holiday, they were to remain in Marldon throughout the war years, and it was only after her mother's death that Elizabeth reluctantly decided to leave the place which they had both grown to love.

They had arrived at Marldon on a wet, misty day and found that their landlady had lit a glowing fire to welcome them, and their first impression of this wooden building poised at the summit of a hill caused them to call it 'The Ark'.* Fortunately for the revival of their spirits, by the next day the mist had rolled away revealing 'every beauty that a pastoral Devon valley knows, woods and farms

---

* Name of bungalow was actually 'Sunnyside'.

and orchards … And along the eastern horizon lay the range of blue hills called Dartmoor.'

Once the decision was taken to stay in Devon, the next step was to look for a permanent home, but finding anything they liked within their purchasing power proved difficult. Then, as Elizabeth wrote, 'there occurred one of those coincidences that are not what they appear'. While looking at a nearby housing development they chanced on a reputable local builder called Mr Clare, who it transpired had a brother at Wells who they also remembered. Hearing of their situation, Mr Clare was anxious to help and built them just the right size little cottage on an overgrown orchard, sited further down the village in the valley known as Westerland. Thanks to him and the kind people of Marldon, they were installed in their new home by the following May—little wonder they called it 'Providence Cottage'.

They stayed in The Ark throughout the winter months and it was a hard time for Elizabeth as she realised how dependent they were now on her writing to help pay for the new house. Her struggle with *The Bird in the Tree* has already been covered. In gratitude to Nanny, who had stayed on with them, she next wrote a children's story dedicated to her.† This book, *Smoky-House*, shows how quickly Elizabeth made use of her new surroundings as the old local pub's name was 'Ye Olde Smokey House'.†† She had probably already heard tales about its history from local characters, and quickly wrote this story of smuggling days in Devon with good triumphing over adversity.

At the beginning of the book Elizabeth writes a description

† The dedication is to 'Nannie', although elsewhere Elizabeth spells the word 'Nanny'.
†† The real inn's name is spelt 'smokey', while the fictional versions in *Smoky-House* and *Gentian Hill* are spelt 'smoky'.

of the village of 'Faraway' which I feel must have echoed her own feelings as spring arrived in Marldon: 'In the village of Faraway everyone was happy, not only in the spring, but always, for Faraway is set in that part of England which is called the West Country, and that is a part of the world so beautiful that the people who live in it are always happy; and as happy people are always kind you could live in the village all your life long and never hear an angry voice or the sound of weeping.'

Later in the book she continued: '… not even when people died, because though Faraway was a long way from the rest of the world it was very close to heaven, so the people in heaven seemed very near.'

Writing about this period Elizabeth later said she and her mother felt the assurance that her father still lived and loved them, and expressed the belief that 'human love at its best is so great a thing that only a God of love could possibly have created it'.

The family living at 'Smoky-House' had the good West Country name of Treguddick, and other characters have suitable names. Five children, the family dogs Spot and Sausage, as well as Mathilda the donkey with an unusually intractable nature, all play their part in the story.

The last chapter, called 'Happy Ever After', gives this assurance to its young readers: 'For generation after generation the sun and the rain and the wind sweep over its round green hills and high moors, and its sheltered wooded valleys. Year after year the moors are painted rose and purple by the sunset, the sheep and cows browse on the slopes of the hills, the primroses come out in the lanes and the birds sing for joy because the spring has come again.'

While some critics were always ready to label Elizabeth's writing as sweet and sugary, knowing of the upheaval some children were experiencing at being evacuated and separated from their families at this time, I would think many of her young readers were helped by this picture of stability and reassurance.

Elizabeth always had a great love for all birds, and her surroundings in Devon gave scope for furthering this interest. When an American, Rose Dobbs, compiled *The Elizabeth Goudge Reader* in 1946, a previously unpublished piece by Elizabeth called 'Dreams' was included. In this Elizabeth told how she would get up at seven o'clock on a dark winter's morning, and after wrestling with a stove which had gone out overnight, put a warm coat on as soon as it was light, and go out to watch the birds flying across the dawn sky. She went on to describe the order in which the birds appeared, and the parts of the garden visited by different species.

In spite of their delight in their new surroundings, the war began to make its impact and Elizabeth recalled how the sound of the cuckoo's call, mingling with the air-raid siren, was to be typical of the intertwining of joy and sorrow that the years spent in Devon brought them.

As well as the demands of her writing, Elizabeth had to struggle with the domestic problems that the war brought to everyone, and those first years must have been far from easy. They had no car or telephone, and she went on the little local bus for shopping at Paignton. The kindness of the village people was something she would never forget, making her observe that 'she never felt so deeply rooted anywhere as in Devon'. It was of course true of all small communities during the war, when people from all backgrounds seemed to be closer. One of the many village characters she mentioned was Bob Patey, who helped in their garden and took Mrs Goudge out in her bath chair through the lovely Devon lanes that reminded her of her Guernsey childhood.

Early in the war, two bombs fell on the field opposite their cottage, jettisoned from a German plane returning home from a raid on the coasts near them. War touched them with news of the death of a cousin on active service and the death of Nanny in a raid on Bath. As the war accelerated, all the lanes and woods in their area were sealed off for use by the American Army awaiting D-Day—this led to more bombs being dropped in the area. After the invasion of Europe took place it was all peaceful again.

Even if they seemed remote from the war, Elizabeth kept abreast with the way it was affecting other sections of the population, as was shown clearly by the creation of the characters in her wartime novel *The Castle on the Hill*, published in 1942. She took a local place, Berry Pomeroy Castle, not far from where she lived, as the setting for the story. She made this the ancestral home of Charles Birley, a distinguished but lonely historian who is joined there by Miss Brown, a casualty from the war, who having lost her home and possessions finds new meaning to her life when she becomes housekeeper at the castle. We are introduced to Mr Isaacson, a Jew forced to flee from Vienna, who is contemplating ending his life until his concern for his landlady's daughters, Moppet and Poppet, whose evacuation to the country has gone awry, leads him to a fresh start in life.

The sentry on guard on Beacon Hill in the story is a link with the one Elizabeth could actually see from her house, and Mr Birley's two nephews, Richard the pilot and Stephen the pacifist, both in love with the same girl, capture the atmosphere of those days in World War 2 when young couples, facing the uncertainties of wartime, felt their feelings intensified as Prunella's thoughts reveal: 'She wanted him with a longing so savage that it shocked her ... Perhaps, she thought, when death stalked the world nature increased the longing of men and women for each other just on purpose, so that they should have babies quickly, while there was time.'

The war was accelerating change in many former values and traditions which Elizabeth conveyed in her descriptions of the two brothers, Richard and Stephen. Despite his privileged background, Richard has very left-wing opinions and tells Prunella he is not fighting for the castle and its traditions but '[f]or the grey-faced men in the streets and the dirty children in the slums. For the factories

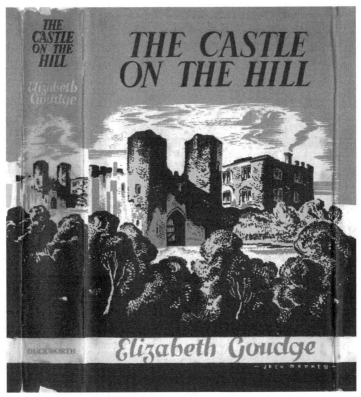

THE FIRST EDITION OF *THE CASTLE ON THE HILL*

and the built-up areas and drunks in the pubs. For the millions of tired drab folk who hurtle backwards and forwards in the tubes and sit on the sands on bank holiday spitting orange peel into the sea. For the jerry-built bungalows that ruin the countryside'.

In none of her writing had Elizabeth ever been so outspoken but even if she was drawing on her late father's opinions, the feelings were ones that many people shared—was 'victory achieved at the cost of mangled children, shrieking women and men shaking in agony …?'

Stephen's painful arguments with Richard and his uncle on his pacifist views left him too weary to mention some of the more interesting theories that Elizabeth has him hold, such as: 'if Napoleon had conquered Wellington England, minus king and aristocracy, might by this time have swung firmly and happily to that Left where Richard felt so at home.' I can't help thinking that some of her readers may have had their allegiance tested when they read that.

The differing views of the two brothers is perhaps brought into perspective when Elizabeth includes a quotation from one of her favourite poets, Keats: 'Patriotism is the glory of making by any means a country happier.'

As expected, *The Castle on the Hill* has a dog appearing on its pages—a gentle Alsatian called Argos, who helps Moppet and Poppet adjust to their very different lives as evacuees at the castle. The purchase of faggots, and the chance to spend their sixpences when Stephen takes them to the nearest town, also boosts their morale.

People had no dishwashers in the 1940s, so the first readers would have identified with the feeling expressed by Miss Brown about the washing-up facing her: 'Though she had been washing up for other people all her life, and supposed she would continue to wash up for them till she rested from it in the grave, she could never get used to the grease of it, the smell of it, the exhaustion of it and its heartbreaking monotony'.

So many details like that appear in the story which for some readers give an accurate historical account of the time, or for others bring back forgotten memories.

The Castle on the Hill was the last novel published by Duckworth. In January 1941 Elizabeth sent a letter to her first publishers explaining her need to change publishers: 'since my father's death, I depend on my books for my living, and I do not feel, under war conditions Duckworth is able to do itself justice, so I feel I must accept Hodder and Stoughton's offer. I am sure you will believe me when I say how sorry I am to make this change.'

The need to be in close contact with her publishers meant Elizabeth was frequently obliged to use the services of the local post office. Her description of the postmistress is so delightful, and so far removed from today's communication network, that it is worth quoting: 'The post office was the front room of her cottage and was filled to the brim with crockery of every sort and kind, china ornaments and great pots of dead flowers. She loved flowers too greatly to throw them away, even when they died, and her room was a mausoleum of flowers. There was a small counter but otherwise little sign that this was a post office, but when you came in to the jangling of the little bell the postmistress would enquire in her lovely voice, "What would you be wanting, Maid?" When you asked for twelve stamps she would look round vaguely, rummage hopelessly among the flowerpots under the counter, and then her face would suddenly brighten and lifting the lid of a teapot she would produce three of the required number. If you wanted to send a telegram (a thing she thought no one in their senses should wish to do) it might be ten minutes before the forms could be found in the recesses of a soup tureen in the fireplace, and then there would be fifteen minutes of struggling with the intricacies of composition and mathematics.'

Between the early phase of the war and the arrival of the pre-invasion forces in Devon, there was a time of comparative calm, and it was during this time that Elizabeth was able to concentrate on finishing the book which was to catapult her into fame. *Green Dolphin Country* was based on the true story of a great-uncle from Guernsey. It was such an extraordinary story that later some readers had difficulty believing it had any true basis.

Writing it over such a long period of time, even during air raids, it had become a very long book and Elizabeth said that finishing it 'nearly killed her'. When you recall how she wrote all her books in longhand, that is not hard to believe and illustrates her tremendous tenacity as well as talent. Fortunately the hard work paid off as her agent in America had entered the book for an MGM Award, and to Elizabeth's astonishment it won with a prize of £30,000.‡

She tells how 'it was a happy nine-days'-wonder in the midst of a horrible war', and the people of Marldon rejoiced wholeheartedly in her success. It's easy to imagine how it became the main topic of conversation in the village for a while—the financiers calculated how much money she would have left after tax and her expenses. We know (because she told us) that she was left with only £4,000, which seems almost to have been a relief to her. The real result of her success, however, was that from then on she was considered 'A BEST SELLER', which meant if not madly rich, the days of her financial worries were behind her.

While I'm sure her friends would have said 'it couldn't happen to a nicer person', the invasion of reporters and pleas for financial help arriving in an avalanche of letters must have been a sore trial to Elizabeth at the time, especially when one determined girl reporter broke in through her bedroom window.

‡ The Metro-Goldwyn-Mayer (MGM) Annual Novel Award, given for the first time in 1944, was worth $125,000 (around £30,000).

I have an interesting copy of a report written by one of these journalists who made the journey to 'a hamlet of 70 souls, which hardly a taxi driver in Torquay has heard of, though Torquay is only four miles away'. This is what she reported about that visit to 'the kindly, nervous, delicate little spinster': 'Different people would advance different reasons why someone from a backwater should write such a novel. Her mother says it is "ancestral memory—My people were all sailors: their blood stirs Elizabeth when she writes of ships."

'Those who know the sense that is talked in a village market place would say only a countrywoman would write: "Three things in chief go to the making of a man or woman into something better than brute beast, and them's the places where life set us down, the folk life knocks us up against, and, not the things ye get, but the things ye don't get".'

She continued: 'Others, like me, who believe genius still to mean capacity for taking pains, might point to Elizabeth Goudge's visits to Exeter County Library, where she ploughed through books on pioneer New Zealand, books on sailing ships, books on Maori battles. It took her 4½ years to write her novel, a few hundred words a day, polished and re-polished.' Our reporter also quoted Mrs Goudge as being 'faintly annoyed because the first book "Island Magic" only brought Elizabeth £30 "and was just as good".'

Green Dolphin Country was later made into a film, but as with many similar ventures, it wasn't thought too satisfactory by its author.‡‡

The action of the story is divided between Guernsey and New Zealand in the mid-19th century. Great-Uncle William had actually gone to Australia, but Elizabeth said she transferred the fictional William to New Zealand because 'her ignorance was greater than of New Zealand'. A note at the front of the book asks lovers of

‡‡ Titled *Green Dolphin Street* to match the US edition of the book, and released in 1947.

New Zealand to excuse any mistakes, though her careful research made the telling of the adventurous years there both convincing and compelling.

In the real story, William had joined the Royal Navy, but after getting into a scrape on shore leave in an eastern port, he failed to return to his ship on time. Knowing this would make him open to a court martial, he deserted, taking another ship to make a new life 'in the New World'. After making good there, but knowing he could not return to Guernsey and the girl he loved, he decided to write to her father asking him to allow her to make the long voyage and come out to marry him. Unfortunately a family weakness for mixing up names (a weakness shared by Mrs Goudge, with less disastrous but amusing results), led him to put the older and less attractive sister's name Marianne instead of Marguerite.

As Marianne was also in love with William, she willingly embarked on the journey. Elizabeth told her readers that William somehow concealed his dismay when she arrived and never told her the truth. How could he when Marianne had come quite alone on the long, stormy voyage—a woman who had never left her safe island home before. He was a compassionate man, married her and made her happy.

This, then, was the basis for the book *Green Dolphin Country*, but who but Elizabeth could have spun it into such a memorable story that was to sell over a million copies all over the world.

In the book the story comes full circle, with Marianne and William returning to Guernsey after 36 years when they are reunited with Marguerite, now the abbess at the convent. Perhaps inevitably, Marianne discovers the truth that has been concealed from her all those years, but in doing so realises William now truly loves her completely.

The book's title is partly derived from the same name as the clipper ship they first knew in the harbour of St Pierre, skippered by the eccentric Captain O'Hara and his faithful seaman Nat, with his one eye and ear, and the parrot, Old Nick. This *Green Dolphin* ship was to take William to New Zealand, and later Marianne, as well as play a significant role in their lives.

It must also be linked with William's first meeting with the lumberman who has lived as a Maori with the name of Tai-Haruru (Sounding Sea). He tells William he has come to 'a country of storms and earthquakes, cannibal country, pioneer country', where he must always be on the alert, for 'we're of value only while the clay that we are holds together; after that, nothingness'. William found this view of life in such complete contrast to that of a missionary, Samuel, whose hospitality he had been given since his arrival in New Zealand, and whose insistence on the immortal soul had become tedious. William decided that for him, there was somewhere between the two, which he considered that free, friendly place, 'Green Dolphin country', which he felt was his special country which Marguerite had once said was 'where our souls find it easiest to escape from self … where what is about us echoes the best that we are'. William decides that for him and the 'two thousand white folk [who] had within this last year come to this country', it could provide just such a place.

This passage gives a good indication of the mixture of romance and adventure found in the book, as well as the philosophical content for which her writing was becoming renowned.

After the success of her book for children, *Smoky-House*, Elizabeth had another published in 1942 called *Henrietta's House*. It was really a sequel to *A City of Bells*, and as such was probably enjoyed as much by her adult readers as children. It was a delightful story which had very favourable reviews here and in America. This may have encouraged her to write another book for children, this time set again in Devon. This book, *The Little White Horse*, published in 1946, was to bring her more prestige when it won the Carnegie Medal for best children's fiction that year.

THE FIRST EDITION OF THE LITTLE WHITE HORSE

She based the adventures in the story around another well-known place near her home, Compton Castle, changing its name to Moonacre Manor. The little white horse that appears to help Maria Merryweather bring about the victory of good over evil, and other magical characters, provided the right ingredients to appeal to children. This would appear to still be so today, as this extract from an Amazon reader suggests: 'I am 13 years old, and I have read masses of books. I was really sorry when I finished the third Harry Potter, but I think *The Little White Horse* is the best book ever.'

The book was published by the University of London Press, and the wonderful illustrations by C. Walter Hodges pleased Elizabeth so much, she dedicated the book to him.

In 1949, her former publishers, Duckworth, came back into her world with a book called *Make-Believe* compiled from short stories about the children in *Island Magic* that Elizabeth had written much earlier.

With all her notable successes Elizabeth did not rest on her laurels and in 1949, another historical novel, *Gentian Hill*, appeared on the bookshelves. It was set in Devon during the Napoleonic Wars. Like *Green Dolphin Country* it is a powerful story of shipwrecks, secret identities, tragedies and reconciliations.

The village name of Marldon where Elizabeth lived was derived from Mergheldon, meaning 'the Hill where the Gentians grow'. After living in the village now for some time and with her love of history, it was not surprising that she chose to show how local interests were caught up with the bigger events of the time. In the aftermath of the war, drawing on the sense of continuity that historical tales gave, Elizabeth was again responding to the feelings of the time.

The story tells how Stella is rescued from a shipwreck and brought up by a couple at Weekaborough Farm. Down the road from Elizabeth, where she possibly went to buy farm produce and may have been invited into the kitchen, was Lower Westerland Farm, and

THE FIRST EDITION OF *GENTIAN HILL*

LOWER WESTERLAND FARM

GENTIAN CLOSE, MARLDON, NAMED AFTER EG'S BOOK, GENTIAN HILL

The endpapers from the first edition of *Gentian Hill*, showing many of the places used in the book

that is where she based her fictional farm with its inviting kitchen: 'All the crannies and bulges of this enchanting cave-like room had unexpected things in them; the bread oven in the thickness of the wall, underneath its fascinating little arch, the grandfather clock, Mother Sprigg's spinning wheel, the warming pans, secret cupboards with home-made wines (and in the very secret cupboards, under the fireplace seats, and in recesses made by removing a few stones from the wall, something even stronger), shelves piled high with pickles and preserves, brass candlesticks and Toby jugs.'

Many places close to Marldon that Elizabeth would have known are incorporated in the story. There is Torre Abbey where, in the story, the Abbé de Colbert celebrates Mass with the Roman Catholics of the area. As his name suggests, he was an aristocratic refugee from France, whose life becomes intertwined with Stella. Stella's sweetheart, Zachary, another orphan because of the French Revolution, has run away from the wretched life of a midshipman, although he returns to take part in the Battle of Trafalgar.

Cockington Court and the nearby Tor Bay appear in the story, together with the legendary St Michael's Chapel which then stood in the bay.

Minor characters are as unforgettable as the main ones, ranging from Sol, the old ploughman who chants to his team as he follows them along the field, quite unaware the chant originated from the monks of the dissolved Torre Abbey, to Granny Bogan, who keeps her mandrake and witchcraft treasures in the priest's cell at Cockington church. There are the usual animals, including Dr Crane's horse, Aesculapius, with its powers of intuition, Hodges the indoor dog, and Daniel the outdoor one.

Regular readers expecting to find spiritual wisdom in the new book were not disappointed. One example being the Bible quotation put in her locket by Stella's French mother, which read: 'Blessed is the man who loves Thee, O God, and his friend in Thee and his enemy for Thee. For he alone loses no one who is dear to him, if all are dear in God, who is never lost.' The locket was to give a vital clue as to Stella's real identity.

Elizabeth dedicated *Gentian Hill* to her cousin Helene who continued visiting them in Devon with her two small children. To Elizabeth's great sorrow, Helene later died in her fifties.

In 1950 Duckworth came up again with another collection of earlier stories under the title of *The Reward of Faith*. The stories were based on Bible stories and legends, and included a story called 'The Three Grey Men' set in Devon: 'The small village tucked away in a fold of the Devon Hills ... did not concern itself much with what was going on in the great world beyond the West Country ... Why should they bother themselves with what went on beyond the confines of their lovely land?' And the story continued about the self-sufficiency of Devon in the days of King Charles I's reign.

As well as the prodigious amount of writing during the years at Devon, increasingly Elizabeth had the task of caring for her mother. Sadly, by the late 1940s this brave woman who had kept cheerful through years of physical suffering, now had to endure the humiliation of mental illness. Although the doctor told Elizabeth it would be too difficult a case to nurse at home, the wonderful support of neighbours and a nurse from the village enabled her to keep her mother at home during that last illness.

After Mrs Goudge died in May 1951, Elizabeth went to stay for the last time at Harewood House, where she said the old house and garden, the sea and marshes were shining in the sun and 'there was healing in the air'.

Before her death Mrs Goudge had urged Elizabeth to remain at Providence Cottage for at least a year, but on her return there from Hampshire, in spite of kind friends visiting and her attempt to resume her writing, everything seemed to have come to a dead end. A wise friend advised her she should have a companion to

141

help her through the winter and suggested someone who might be interested. Reluctantly Elizabeth decided to follow this advice and wrote to Jessie Monroe.

Many years later Elizabeth wrote, 'it was the most wonderful event that ever happened to me. Jessie was a lover of the outdoors, with a passion for gardening'. Jessie recalled to me with some amusement how, when some local friends were being entertained to meet her at Providence Cottage, and when in the course of conversation she admitted she had read none of Elizabeth's books, a ghastly hush fell on the assembly. It didn't matter to Elizabeth one jot, but one difference that did take them both a while to adjust to was their religious outlook, with Elizabeth describing Jessie as 'a fiery Celtic Presbyterian, brought up on *Foxe's Book of Martyrs*'.

Fortunately, right from the start, a mutual love of dogs was recognised, which resulted in their acquiring a Dandie Dinmont puppy which, as Elizabeth was reading about the Kon Tiki expedition at the time, they called Tiki. She was to happily share their lives for the next ten years.

Ever since the death of her mother, relatives had been urging Elizabeth to move nearer to them, but it was only when Jessie, after a very wet winter, made it clear she would welcome moving to a place where gardening would be easier than the wet, heavy soil of Devon, that Elizabeth went along with the idea. It wasn't easy, for her love of Devon was deeply rooted and I think her decision to move shows how concern for others often outweighed her own preferences.

Writing in her autobiography twenty years after leaving Devon, she confessed that 'although happy in her new home, waves of homesickness for the West Country would sweep over her as she missed the running streams, high hills and wild places'.

Before moving Elizabeth had started writing another novel with another Devonshire background. *The Rosemary Tree* wasn't published until 1956, but as the story does not depend on its setting like *Gentian Hill*, it can be looked at later. A children's book called *Linnets and Valerians*, published in 1964, is definitely placed back in Devon.§ Elizabeth stayed with friends back in Devon in the early 1960s while Jessie was recovering from a back injury, and possibly it was this visit which reminded her of local folktales, prompting her to include them in a book about witches and magical happenings in the village of High Barton. The fictional village where the four children—the Linnets—have their adventures bears a close resemblance to Marldon.

Delightful characters such as Ezra, the one-legged gardener who talks to his bees, Lady Alicia with her pet monkey Abednego, together with the hair-raising adventures, make this another unforgettable book for her young readers. Elizabeth said she enjoyed writing for children and that sense of enjoyment is very apparent.

As with the other places she had lived, Elizabeth kept in touch with friends in Devon and was saddened at the changes that 'progress' brought to the lovely places she had known in the county. In 1974 she wrote, 'Devon, as I knew it when I lived there thirty years ago, before almost all the county became a holiday playground and the fairies fled, was an unearthly place. The round green hills where the sheep grazed, the wooded valleys and the lanes full of wild flowers, the farms and apple orchards were all full of magic, and the birds sang in that long-ago Devon as I have never heard them singing anywhere else in the world; in the spring we used to say it sounded as though the earth itself was singing'.

Her readers can be glad that her love for the Devon countryside resulted in books that captured it before it changed for ever. The

§ The book has also been published in the UK with an alternative title, *The Runaways*.

THE FIRST EDITION OF *LINNETS AND VALERIANS*

isolation and comparative peacefulness during her years there enabled her to write many of her best-loved books there.

Sadly those years took a considerable toll on her heath, with arthritis causing limited mobility.

When she left Devon it was as a famous worldwide author, receiving mail from readers everywhere, many telling her of their personal problems which she always tried to answer. Fortunately, Jessie Monroe remained with Elizabeth in the following years, acting as a shield from the more intrusive public, which might otherwise have limited her time for writing.

THE FIRST US EDITION OF *THE REWARD OF FAITH*

THE SMOKEY HOUSE INN

MARLDON CHURCH

DEVON FOOTSTEPS

I decided to use Paignton as my base for my 'Footsteps in Devon' journey. It was the nearest town to Marldon and one used frequently for shopping expeditions by Elizabeth.

In *Gentian Hill* Elizabeth gave an interesting description of the town as it would have been to people of those times: 'Paignton was much older than Torquay and looked upon the lovely little place with its flowery Strand as a mere upstart. Paignton was famous for several things, its cabbages, its beautiful fifteenth century church, and the Palace of the Bishop of Exeter standing in a great meadow beside the church … it was a place of tranquillity and peace; and so was the old harbour, with thatched cottages clustered about it.' Both the shipwrecks in the story of *Gentian Hill* were based on true events that took place on the rocks of Paignton Ledge.

Today Paignton is a busy seaside resort, better known for its zoo and steam railway than for cabbages and church buildings. Although it can no longer be described as a place of tranquillity, I found it a pleasant place to stay during a week of May sunshine.

Fortunately the local network of small buses linking it with surrounding villages still operates a frequent service, and enabled me to visit Marldon in this way.

Following directions from friendly fellow passengers, I left the bus at a junction where I was told the road down the hill led to the old village of Marldon. How would it compare to the time when Sol and Stella trod the same way? 'The lane led downhill again to the village of Gentian Hill, lying in a secluded valley. This valley

147

was another little kingdom all to itself, quite different in character to Weekaborough [Lower Westerland Farm], for there was no break in the hills which surrounded it through which one could see the moors or the sea, and through which the fresh winds could blow, so that the trees were not bent by the winds as in the Weekaborough valley, and the flowers came out earlier and were more luxuriant. In hot weather it could be very sultry down in Gentian Hill, and in wet weather, when the stream that ran down the side of the village street overflowed, it was often flooded.

'But it was a beautiful village, surrounded with orchards, its thatched cob cottages set in gardens packed tight with flowers, the low stone walls that surrounded them cascading with green ferns. The beautiful old church with its tall tower crowned the knoll that gave the village its name, and gentians grew in the churchyard. Grouped about the church were the Church House Inn, the Parsonage, Dr Crane's house, the forge and the village shop.'

It was still quite early in the morning as I followed their path down the hill to Marldon village. Everywhere seemed deserted, except for one old gentleman, who greeted us courteously and, in answer to my query, said he remembered Elizabeth Goudge, and said she had lived at the other end of the village, though he didn't know exactly where. Reaching the foot of the village I found a group of old cottages before arriving at the Church House Inn, but that was still closed and there was no shop or forge to be seen. Climbing up the incline through the churchyard with its old yew trees, towards the square-towered church, I was pleased to find it open and passed through the porch where Zachary had noticed the proclamation urging men to come forward in defence of their country.

In her preface to *Gentian Hill*, Elizabeth had written that she gave the church a vicar, even though at that time it was served by a church in Paignton. The notes about the church tell that it wasn't until 1912 that the church had its own vicar, but as I rested in the pew it seemed a good time to read again the delightful passage about the fictional parson, for in many of her novels there are other clergymen who epitomise the varying positions they held in the society of their own time.

'No one could have called Parson Ash a spiritual looking man. He was short and fat, with a round, pink and exceedingly shrewd face, twinkling black boot-button eyes and a rollicking laugh and smile. He rode to hounds with a verve astonishing in a man nearer seventy than sixty, and was a good shot. He was a bachelor, and as the younger son of an aristocratic family, who had put him into the church because they did not know what else to do with him, was well off. He was hospitable, kept an excellent table and a good cellar. He could carry his drink well and tell a good story. He performed his duty, as he saw it, excellently, never forgetting a christening, wedding or funeral and getting through the ceremony in record time. He saw to it that his church was clean, his churchyard tidy, his clerk and band punctual. He himself was always well-dressed in well-brushed clerical black with white bands, an old-fashioned white cauliflower wig and a jaunty black shovel hat. He did not personally visit the sick, for fear of infection, nor the bereaved because grief depressed him, but he sent them soup and port wine by the hand of his housekeeper, and if he caught little boys thieving he beat them good and hard. The village was proud of him and liked him. He minded his own business, let them mind theirs, and never preached a long sermon.'

I found it rather amusing after that to read in the current church magazine that they were hoping to soon appoint a new priest to the parish. I doubt, if Parson Ash were applying, whether he would have much to offer today's selectors for that post.

I read in the notes about the history of the church that there were once two galleries at the west end of the church—one for the schoolchildren and one for the musicians—and that both were taken down in 1885 to make room for an organ. Again the description given in *Gentian Hill* of how the music would have been at the services here in the 18th century was too good to miss recalling at this point of my journey.

'If it was an unholy din it was hearty and greatly enjoyed. There was not a man, woman or child who did not sing at the top of its voice; unless otherwise engaged in the gallery blowing or sawing away at bugle, trombone, clarinet, trumpet, flute, fiddle or bass viol … expending their last ounce of breath and strength upon the final deafening chord, and everyone sank back exhausted, yet smiling with a sense of duty done.'

Reading in the magazine about present-day activities in the village, I had the feeling that the friendly village atmosphere, whether in the 18th century or the 20th, which had endeared it to Elizabeth, was still alive and thriving in the present day. Back in the village a notice telling of some social event to be held at 'the Smokey Inn' reminded me there was still much to be explored. Everywhere was still deserted, so chance of obtaining transport seemed rather bleak, until I spotted a young woman with a small child coming from one of the cottages towards a car parked outside. She was going up to the top of the village and kindly agreed to drop me at Ye Olde Smokey House.

Unfortunately, licensing hours meant that too was still closed, and there was no one about to question. It now looks a very respectable establishment, as does the surrounding part of the village, but according to the description given of it in *Gentian Hill*, this was not so in the 18th century, when we are told it was 'a secondary village, separated from Gentian Hill proper by a hill crowned by a small dense wood, Hangman's Wood … There a group of very old cottages lurched drunkenly in the midst of gay untidy gardens … and the whole gay, disreputable group of cottages was known briefly as Smoky.

'The people who lived at Gentian Hill had mostly lived there for generations, and seldom left their homes, but the Smoky people were a shifting population, sometimes there and sometimes not. The Excise men always had their eye on Smoky, and so had the gamekeepers of the neighbouring estates. Gentian Hill always spoke with patronising disapproval of Smoky, but never gave it away. There were certain homes in Gentian Hill where a Smoky man in trouble knew he would not be refused a welcome and a hiding place, and few among the more well-to-do cottages whose secret cupboards had not got their secret store of French brandy and tobacco'.

Whether Elizabeth got her information from old records or tales passed on by the local people, it makes for interesting reading.

Having been told I could board the little bus again which would take me round the village to the local post office, I decided I would have to leave 'Smokey' without obtaining any further information about its darker past.

So, passing mostly modern houses en route, the driver put me off opposite the post office, where I hoped to be given directions to Providence Cottage where Elizabeth had lived in the 1940s. The present post office bore no resemblance to the one Elizabeth knew and, like many today, combined its post office services with that of a small store. It was quite busy, with two queues, so I joined the one for the main counter. When it was my turn to be served I paid for some cards and asked the assistant if she had heard of Elizabeth Goudge. Before she could answer, several ladies from the other queue chipped in telling me that they did indeed know about her and would be happy to help. They were all very well meaning, but I soon got a bit confused, as they seemed to be suggesting it was a bungalow called 'Gentian Cottage' 'just round the corner' that I needed, while Providence Cottage drew a blank. One lady told me how she had read *Gentian Hill* years ago, while living elsewhere, and had never dreamt she would one day be living there—she had been trying, unsuccessfully, to grow gentians ever since. They all seemed to know about the *Gentian Hill* book, but were a bit vague about the others.

Fortunately, one of my new acquaintances lived just across the road, and offered us hospitality in her bungalow, while I sorted out the information I'd been given. She explained that like most of the other ladies, she was a comparative newcomer, but that next door there was a longstanding local person who could possibly help, and as this same lady ran a taxi service, this proved to be a great suggestion.

Refreshed, thanks to our generous friend, we set off with her neighbour, who had been briefed about our enquiries. We turned right at the crossroads towards the part known as Westerland, and pulled in fairly soon to a small lane, from which we got our first glimpse of Providence Cottage. 'Yes, it belonged to Mrs Johnston, who she knew well and she would give us her 'phone number later.'

My query as to the whereabouts of Lower Westerland Farm meant we soon took a left turn onto a quieter road, and pulled up opposite a large building which backed onto the other side of the road. Now tiled, our driver said it would have once been thatched as was Weekaborough in *Gentian Hill*. Continuing along this quiet lane, bordered by flowery verges, we turned again into more wooded countryside, which led to Berry Pomeroy Castle.

The gateway and ruins which greet you are most impressive. The castle has been owned by the Seymour family since 1548, when they purchased it from the Pomeroy family. They in turn had owned it since the Norman Conquest. It is now managed by English Heritage who open it to the public. Little wonder that the mystery of the deserted mansion built by the Seymours within the castle walls intrigued Elizabeth so that her imagination used it to create a home for her wartime characters. In causing it to be destroyed in an air raid, she restored it to historical accuracy as a ruin again by the end of the book. Today the castle is very much on the tourist route, and is famous for the hauntings in many parts of the castle, said to be seen by many over the years.

Next our helpful driver drove us back through Marldon to go to

Cockington Court and church, which also featured in *Gentian Hill*. Our route took us through lovely leafy lanes, with wonderful scents wafting in the open windows from the spring flowers that grew all along the way, but it was time to part with our driver, and explore this area at our leisure. Just how Elizabeth would have reached Cockington in wartime is not clear, but by the descriptions she gave, it's obvious she must have known it well. Here is how she gave the account of Stella's first visit there with Mrs Loraine: 'They drove on through Cockington village with its whitewashed thatched cottages and its fourteenth century forge with a large pond in front of it … The church and almshouses as well as the manor were within the park and visitors to them might drive through it when they pleased … The manor was a beautiful three-storied house with a courtyard in front of it.'

Although there is no denying that Cockington is now one of the main tourist attractions in the area, the splendour of its setting in grounds fringed with lovely old trees, ensures it remains a delightful place to visit. On a warm day in May, I was pleased to avail myself of one of the attractions on offer, and ride round the estate, which consists of 287 acres, in one of the horse-drawn carriages. These have been a feature of Cockington for the last seven years, and on the previous day the annual horse-blessing ceremony had been held. Certainly the animals looked in fine shape at the beginning of the season.

The forge has been converted to a gift shop, but the pond remains near where the horses assemble. Other village buildings are now used to provide other amenities for the visitors. Cockington Court is little changed externally, and the house said to have begun life in 1068 when the site was granted to William de Falaise, who had fought at the side of William I, remains a serene looking building.

Stella's first visit to Cockington was to visit Granny Bogan at one of the almshouses, taking presents of a flannel petticoat, and packets of tea, peppermint and sugar. The account of the acceptance of the presents gives what I like to call a 'Goudgian gem': Granny Bogan 'sounded grateful but not obsequiously so. If the gentry liked to bestow charity upon the poor, let them. It pleased them and did no harm.'

Stella's next encounter with Granny Bogan is early on a midsummer morning, when she is taken by Granny Bogan into the church where she keeps 'her treasure' hidden in a room in the church tower. First we have Stella looking at the main part of the church and noticing the beautiful carved screen, with the sixteen carved birds, feeding on a vine. She also noticed the lovely stained-glass windows, with pictures of the saints.

Halfway up the tower, Granny Bogan takes her into a cell-like room, where in a cupboard within a fireplace, she reveals two books and a mandrake root, which Stella knew was used by witches. One book contains spells she has collected, and the other is an ancient manuscript written in Latin. She insists that Stella now have her treasure, and it is not hard to guess that the manuscript when translated by the Abbé, will relate to the legend of St Michael's Chapel, which readers have already heard mentioned.

Reading the guide to this old Church of St George and St Mary, I learnt that it did not become the parish church of Cockington until 1881, so during the late 18th century it would just have served as a chapel for the village. There has never been a graveyard attached to the church, and in pre-Reformation times, was linked to the nearby Torre Abbey. These facts make the account in the book far more credible.

It is now a beautifully maintained church, holding regular services. The rood screen admired by Stella was skilfully restored in 1920, so the description in the book bears more resemblance to the way Elizabeth would have seen it on her visits, than its former state. Much of the present-day stained glass is modern—the present east window replacing one destroyed by a bomb in 1943. On the west side, however, some 15th-century glass remains, showing the figures mentioned by Stella, of St John, St Andrew, St James and St Peter. Another window, also on the west side, has 14th-century glass thought to be St Martin with a sword, as Stella noted.

The tower chamber with the fireplace, where Granny Bogan hid her treasure, is now used as a ringing chamber.

The church contains memorials to the Carey and Mallock families, showing how Elizabeth wove fact with fiction, as she admitted in the foreword to *Gentian Hill*.

Torre Abbey is now open to the public, and provides an assortment of attractions within its grounds. Although St Michael's Chapel in Tor Bay has disappeared, the bay itself, which has witnessed fleets assembled in its waters from Napoleonic days to the Second World War, now only provides moorings for peaceful sailing vessels.

There remained one more place associated with Elizabeth's writing in Devon, and that is Compton Castle, a mile away from Marldon, and the setting for *The Little White Horse*. It was given to the National Trust by the Gilbert family in 1951. It had been in their family for six hundred years, and is among the few fortified houses to survive without later alterations and additions. The old well where, in the story, the Norman princess hid her pearls, can still be seen. No wonder this old place steeped in history struck Elizabeth as a good place to set the struggle between the forces of good and evil, in her children's book.

In the church at Marldon there were several memorials to the Gilbert family, who were responsible for many additions to the church over the centuries, and Elizabeth may have known members of the family who still lived at the castle.

It is interesting to realise that in wartime, when travel was restricted, Elizabeth found within a few miles' radius of her home, enough material to inspire several books.

The highlight of my journey to Devon was to be invited to visit Providence Cottage to meet Mrs Johnston who had bought it from Elizabeth in 1951, and lived there ever since.

Travelling again on the little bus to Marldon, I was instructed to alight at the crossroads and follow the road towards Westerland, but then turn into a lane on the left which would bring me round to the gate of the cottage.

As the road is now a very busy one, this was good advice. The lane was another typical Devon lane, with bluebells, campions, and wild strawberries growing along its banks. Again the lovely scents as we walked along the damp path under the trees, made it a memorable experience. No wonder these Devon lanes reminded Mrs Goudge of the water lanes she had known in her childhood in Guernsey. I doubt if the lane had changed much since Elizabeth knew it, which made it a memorable way to approach the house where she had lived.

Mrs Johnston greeted us cordially and led us into the cottage. She had bought it at auction for £3,800, and said she had made very few alterations since—just an extension to the entrance porch, and a new exit from the lounge. She agreed that Mr Clare had indeed built it very well and she had loved living in it all this time. She brought up her family there and for a long time had been a well-known breeder of Corgi dogs which keeps her busy—one of her dogs had just had a litter of seven pups.

We talked in the large spacious lounge, with lovely views towards Dartmoor. The cottage has just two bedrooms, but there is also an attic room. It has a lovely peaceful atmosphere, comfortably furnished with plenty of bookcases.

Mrs Johnston remembered Elizabeth very well and found her a charming person, although at the time, she thought her older than 51, as her hair was white and she obviously suffered from arthritis. She recalled there were no shops in the village during her first years there, but could remember many village characters who have sadly passed away.

The front garden is mostly grassed and slopes slightly down to the entrance. There was a big vegetable garden when she bought the cottage, and she understood the Goudges' gardener was 'a real vegetable man'. She agreed the soil could be difficult, as Jessie had soon discovered after her first attempts at gardening there.

When they met, Elizabeth told her how pleased she was that someone with children and dogs was going to live at the cottage. It's true, when we are forced to move from somewhere we love, we like to think we are handing it over to someone suitable.

Mrs Johnston told me that she also believed that Elizabeth had been very generous after becoming successful, and that she had bought a bungalow in the village for the couple who had worked for them as housekeeper and chauffeur. This apparently was the 'Gentian Cottage' that the ladies at the post office had thought I was looking for. Sadly she said the lady there had only died very recently—another interesting link sadly lost. Apparently the wooden building christened 'The Ark', where the Goudges had first lived in Marldon, can no longer be easily identified, as the timber walls are now rendered over.† In the early years of living at Providence Cottage, Mrs Johnston recalled how she had many people calling, wanting to see where 'their favourite author' had lived. She especially remembered one American lady who was overcome with emotion, saying how blessed she felt to be there. There were even mystery coach tours, which would pause to let the occupants peer over the hedge—disconcerting if they were sunbathing.

It was a lovely sunny day when I visited Providence Cottage, but having previously seen the large clergy house where they had lived

† According to the Marldon Local History Group website, it is a bungalow now known as 'St Anthony' on the Totnes Road at Marldon Cross Hill.

earlier, I can well understand that, whatever the weather, owning and living in this little cottage must have given Elizabeth and her mother great joy in their last years together.

After my short stay in Devon, I could understand Elizabeth's reluctance to leave, but felt very grateful that with the passing of fifty years, I had still managed to experience for myself some of the magic of the Devon that had inspired her writing.

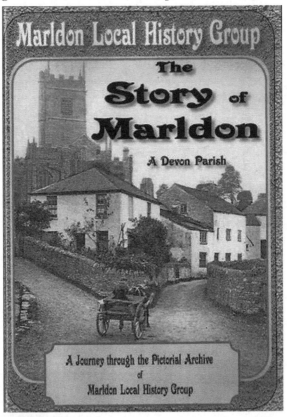

A DVD PRODUCED BY THE MARLDON LOCAL HISTORY GROUP

TWO VIEWS OF MARLDON CHURCH

ELIZABETH GOUDGE IN HER BEDROOM AT ROSE COTTAGE
(USED IN THE FIRST EDITION OF *WEG*)

THE REWARDING YEARS

ROSE COTTAGE 1952–1970

In those days, Peppard Common could still be said to be in the country. A few houses were grouped around it and to the north the road that crossed the common disappeared towards Henley between tall elm trees, the village pond to the left and the seventeenth-century inn, The Dog, to the right. The entrance to Dog Lane could hardly be seen where it left the road beside the inn, and the two cottages in the lane hiding behind the inn could hardly be seen either. Dog Lane is very ancient, it was a Pack and Prime lane and is still called that when it reaches Henley. The two cottages are called Primrose Cottage and Rose Cottage and have been called by those names for perhaps three hundred years.

Our lives often appear to go round in circles. When Elizabeth arrived at Reading station at the end of her journey from Devon, that is what she must have felt was happening to her. It was over thirty years since she had first arrived there to study at the Reading School of Art, living with cousins in the town. Now she was again to stay with one of the same cousins while she searched for a property to buy in the area.

For some time nothing suitable came along, until one day, reading the local paper she spotted a notice of a 17th-century cottage for sale in the small hamlet of Peppard Common. It was a quiet, unspoilt location, about six miles from Reading and four miles from Henley-on-Thames. As soon as she saw Rose Cottage, situated in

Dog Lane, she knew her search was over. The cottage had recently been restored and it stood in a garden large enough to give scope to Jessie's gardening activities and for Tiki's games.

Dog Lane was an ancient track where men with pack horses used to ride up from Henley, laden with goods. They would pass Rose Cottage and Primrose Cottage before reaching the main road and The Dog Inn. Rose Cottage had once belonged to the Rectory coachman—he was succeeded by his daughter who had lived there for fifty years. Before the days of washing machines and laundries, she had been the village washerwoman, using the little room that now adjoined the lounge for her work. In the recent restoration her former kitchen and parlour had been made into one big room, retaining the old beams and the original fireplaces at each end.

It was at the former kitchen end that Elizabeth was often aware of 'a presence' during her first years at the cottage. Tiki also would growl, looking at the corner where perhaps the old lady had sat in her rocking chair by the fire. Visitors too were sometimes aware of an odd feeling around that area. Elizabeth said it disappeared after a few years, so perhaps the old lady became happy with their occupation of her cottage.

Many old cottages within reach of Henley, including Rose Cottage, were thought to have been built using old ship's timbers— on hot days Elizabeth noticed the smell of spices emanating from the old beams.

Rose Cottage was to provide a peaceful home for the rest of Elizabeth's life, enabling her to continue writing successfully for many more years. Jessie made a delightful old-world garden, replanting many of the kind of flowers that would have grown there earlier. In the field around the cottage, horses, cows, sheep and lambs often grazed, and gypsies sometimes set up camp, providing Elizabeth with material for a story.

The cottage had two bedrooms, with Elizabeth's becoming

ALL SAINTS' CHURCH, PEPPARD

known as the ship's captain's room because of its shape and the old ship's beams in it. From the back window she could see the spire of Peppard church.

Although Elizabeth grew to love the cottage, she never felt so at home with the surrounding area as she had with Devon, describing it as 'too civilised and parklike, with no running streams, high hills or wilderness'.

Her arthritis probably meant she did not get as involved with the local community as she had earlier, and with Jessie now able to undertake the responsibilities which had been hers when her mother was alive, she was able to take life at a more leisurely pace. Excusing her withdrawal from social life because of the demands of her writing, I feel it could have been more that her natural inclination for solitude was something for the first time she could indulge. She had a good ally in Jessie, who understood the need to protect her from unwanted intrusion. After the trauma of her mother's death and moving house it is good to know she had the first few years at Rose Cottage without the former financial pressure to keep writing.

It wasn't until after the publication of *The Rosemary Tree* in 1956 that the pattern of writing a new book every two years became re-established.

As we have noted, Elizabeth began *The Rosemary Tree* while still at Devon, and used places there for the setting of the story with the fictional 'Silverbridge' probably being Totnes, while 'Belmaray Manor', where the rosemary bush grew, seems much like Bowden House. The story begins in the spring which leads me to think that part was written during Elizabeth's last few months there before moving.

Written after her mother's death, this new book shows a subtle change in the portrayal of its characters. As well as descriptions of their physical appearance, as we meet each character, a glimpse

FIRST EDITION OF *THE ROSEMARY TREE*

into their past lets us understand better why they have become the person they are now.

Although one of the hallmarks of Elizabeth's writing had always been her empathy with other people's lives, this fresh insight possibly arose from no longer having her mother to discuss things with, and so led to her thinking more deeply into what had previously influenced the characters she created.

The first example in *The Rosemary Tree* of this new perception is Harriet, the former nanny to the Wentworth family, now so crippled with arthritis she is confined to life in her room and is now dependent on them for care. She feels herself useless, but as the story unfolds we are aware that her love and thought for them plays an invaluable role in their lives.

Another was John Wentworth, the vicar of Belmaray, who, after a nerve-racking wartime experience, considers he is ineffectual, both as a priest and husband. As his kindness and understanding towards others is depicted in the story, it becomes obvious this is not so. His abrasive wife, Daphne, and his three daughters all depend on John's help in resolving their difficulties, while the unloved teacher Miss Giles owes a second chance to his thoughtfulness.

Other strands of the story, from the bitterness of the ex-prisoner Michael to the slothfulness of Mrs Belling, illustrate this new dimension of her characters.

Seemingly insignificant passages can point out truths that might otherwise pass unnoticed. My copy of *The Rosemary Tree* previously belonged to a deceased aunt who, for many years after the death of their parents, had devoted her life to her brother in much the same way as Maria had to Richard in the story—both couples being happy in a situation which relatives and others found incomprehensible. Had my aunt identified with Maria as she read this passage in the book? 'Splendid as had been the love between them, that lifelong love of a brother and sister that at its greatest can be almost deeper than that of husband and wife, they had never spoken to each other very intimately either of their love or of Richard's afflictions. Their generation had never felt the need of having their exact spiritual, emotional, nervous and physical state, as conceived by themselves, thoroughly understood by those about them.'

Not all the critics were enthusiastic about the book, considering that the deepening spirituality of her work would not bode well for her future success. I don't imagine this worried Elizabeth, as long as her readers were satisfied. Life at Rose Cottage had settled into a pleasant, quiet routine, with Elizabeth sharing Jessie's pleasure as the garden took shape with the older plants, shrubs and trees, making a wonderful haven for the birds. Knowing that the original 17th-century garden would have had a herb garden, Jessie felt it was important to recreate that as well.

Elizabeth was to draw on Jessie's expertise about herbs and their use when she started to write her next book, *The White Witch*, dedicating it to her when it was finished. Published in 1958, by Hodder and Stoughton, it is set in the period of the English Civil War, showing how allegiance to one side or the other in that conflict divided friends and families. Much of the action in the book is again centred quite close to where Elizabeth lived, with her thorough research into that period of history making it a compelling narrative.

The gypsies who camped on the field behind the house also inspired Elizabeth to study their lifestyle and beliefs which she incorporated into the story, and an 'experience' she had, soon after moving into Rose Cottage, fired her imagination to also weave that into this unusual story. This is how she described it: 'Some little while after I had moved into the Oxfordshire cottage where I live now, I was trying hard to love it (a difficult process because my roots were still in the earth of Devonshire), when an impulse sent me to the window of the sitting room. It was spring, and cold, but the air had that special quality of a cold spring, the coldness of living water, and was scented with the wild violets that grew in clumps about the old garden, and over the sweetbriar hedge to the field beyond, and feeling the first twinges of love for the place, when a woman came down the narrow path in front of the window. She came from the place where the path ended abruptly in the hedge and I was told later that there used to be a gate there leading to the lane. Her name was Froniga ... Some while later, after I had time to absorb the beauties of my new home, I wrote something of her history and that of her cottage in a book called *The White Witch*. How accurate it is I have no way of knowing since only the last sixty years of the life of the cottage is known and Froniga lived in the seventeenth century.'

We first meet Froniga in the story when she is bringing a basket of 'strewing herbs, consisting of lavender, germander, pennyroyal and rosemary from her garden'. We learn that Froniga is half gypsy, and half gentry and that '[s]he made ointments and lotions and medicines for the sick ... [Her garden] was a fragrant and musical place, humming with bees, with grass paths separating the cushions and knots and parterres of colour and scent. Froniga had more than a hundred herbs and knew all their names and just where to find them ... Among her flowers were marigolds, paggles, daisies and gilliflowers ... She grew her roses chiefly for medicinal purposes but for their beauty too; apothecary and rosa-mundi, velvet and village maid, damask roses for making melrosette [a popular drink], the musk rose for its scent ... Of sweetbriar roses she grew a quantity, both for metheglyn and toilet waters. They hedged her whole domain as well as the herb garden and the cottage was named after them ... Violets grew under the cottage wall ... She could never have enough of them for conserves and jellies, and as an excellent medicine for hang-over.'

The description of the cottage is also fascinating: 'The parlour, like the kitchen, had a stone-flagged floor and whitewashed walls,

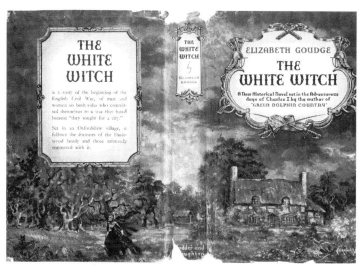

FIRST EDITION OF *THE WHITE WITCH*, COTTAGE MODELLED ON ROSE
COTTAGE (SEE BACK COVER FOR FULL PICTURE)
TOP WINDOW WAS THAT OF EG'S BEDROOM

and from the low beams that crossed the ceiling hung bunches of herbs. A log fire burned here too, for Froniga infused her herbs over its heat, and her patients liked to sit on the bench before it while they told her how poorly they felt. There was an oak table where she sat to do her work, and two presses where she kept all her medicines and lotions, ointments, comfits and preserves.'

Elizabeth said she enjoyed writing this book, and this shows in the confident way she combined fictional and historical characters to make the story so convincing.

It showed how the Puritan resolve to upset what they considered to be idolatrous forms of worship, led to much unhappiness, and affected even the small parish churches like the one Parson Hawthyn had in his care. With Squire Haslewood being a newly converted and zealous Puritan, he was ordered to strip his little church of everything that offended the new beliefs. Remaining 'an obstinate royalist', the parson wanted his flock to remember this Christmas, and worship in the way he had taught them, believing by next year he would have been driven from his church, so he disobeyed the Squire and the church was decorated with holly and ivy and the beautiful little wood carvings that he made. Parson Hawthyn made clear he considered the fanatical Puritan's God was the tribal God of the Israelites, who had forgotten the mercy of Christ.

Although Robert Haslewood did his best to wreck the Christmas worship, he attended the service and listened while Parson Hawthyn used a prayer by Archbishop Laud which acknowledged the church could go astray: 'Bless O Gracious Father, Thine Holy Catholic Church. Fill it with truth and grace. Where it is corrupt, purge it, where it is in error direct it; where it is superstitious rectify it; where it is amiss reform it; where it is right strengthen and confirm it; where it is divided and rent asunder heal the breaches of it. O Thou Holy one of Israel.'

When it came to the sermon, Parson Hawthyn again tried to be tactful and said that because he believed in times of conflict and emotion, men often spoke words they are sorry for after, he would instead repeat a portion of a sermon by John Donne on the subject of mercy—adding, 'I bid you listen carefully, for in all the sorrow and conflict of our day there is one thing, and one thing only, which never fails us, and that is the mercy of God'. The sermon ended with the words: 'One of the most convenient hieroglyphics of God is a circle, and a circle is endless. Whom God loves He loves to the end; and not only to their own end, to their death, but to His end; and His end is, that He might love them still.'

Elizabeth keeps this theme of mercy throughout the book, whether for Puritans or gypsies, while the character of Yoben, recusant priest, and royalist spy in the disguise of a gypsy, in love with Froniga, who gives up his life in place of another, is surely one that only Elizabeth could make us believe in.

Talking to a journalist after the publication of *The White Witch*, Elizabeth said: 'You can have a story in your brain beating to come out—or a certain character for whom you feel quite deeply. Your characters take over absolutely. I plan it out for them in the beginning, but they won't keep to it. I become obsessed with some character who comes into my mind. I didn't mean to write about this house, but I believe a woman came in through the gate at the end of this path and that I saw her walk past and she was Froniga, the heroine of "The White Witch". Whether I saw a ghost or imagined the whole thing I don't know. The first year we were here the gypsies were camping on the field. I had never met any real gypsies before and in those days they had painted caravans and sang round the camp fires. There was an amazing old grandmother and I would look up and see this marvellous old face smiling at me through the kitchen window while I was doing the washing up—she went into my book just as she was (Madona).'

Having to do local research for the book possibly helped her at last to put Devon and her life there in the past where it belonged, and start to enjoy the rewards from her writing that life in her new home was bringing.

Certainly she now felt ready to undertake a book which had been in her mind for some time, a life of St Francis of Assisi—a difficult and demanding work which will be looked at in the chapter about her religious writing.

Soon after the publication of *Saint Francis of Assisi* in 1959, their first dog Tiki's short span of life ended. As all dog lovers know, heartbreak every ten years is hard to take. Tiki had been an outdoor dog, but his successor, Randa, was the opposite, not liking to get her feet wet. Randa too was to share their lives for a further ten years.

In writing her next book, *The Dean's Watch*, Elizabeth was to look back to the years she had lived in Ely. She said the book had been at the back of her mind waiting for the right time. Now a quiet time at the cottage suggested it was the time to do it. As well as using her memories of Ely, she went back thirty years to a couple she still remembered seeing at a Gray's Inn ball, dressed in 18th-century costume.

A family heirloom also seems to have played a part in the inspiration for the story. Giving an interview to a French journalist (her books had been popular in France since the early years of her career), Elizabeth showed her a beautiful old silver watch in a sphere-shaped watchcase, saying 'C'est le souvenir de famille qui m'a inspirée'.

From all these, Elizabeth constructed another 'best-seller' which was to be one of her own as well as her readers' favourites, but even with all her memories to help, she must have done considerable research about clocks and watches to be able to write so authoritatively about them in her book.

Readers not too impatient to start on the story had their attention caught by a delightful epitaph to a former watchmaker, taken from a churchyard at Lydford, at the front of the book: 'Here lies in a horizontal position the outside case of

GEORGE ROUTLEDGE, WATCHMAKER

Integrity was the mainspring and prudence
the regulator of all the actions of his life;
humane, generous and liberal,
His hand never stopped till he had relieved distress.

So nicely regulated were his movements that
he never went wrong, except when set going
by people who did not know his key.
Even then he was easily set right again.
He had the art of disposing of his time so well,
till his hours glided away, his pulse
stopped beating.

He ran down, November 14th, 1801, aged 57
In hopes of being taken in hand by his Maker
Thoroughly cleaned, repaired, wound up, and
set going in the world to come,
when time shall be no more.'

We meet Isaac Peabody, the watchmaker, in the first chapter where he is described as 'a round-shouldered little man with large feet and a great domed and wrinkled forehead', and a white straggling beard. 'His eyes were very blue beneath their shaggy eyebrows and chronic indigestion had crimsoned the tip of his button nose'.

Isaac lived in Angel Lane, with his embittered sister Emma, where he not only mended watches, including the Dean's, but having served a seven-year apprenticeship in London with the Clockmaker's

Company, was always making a clock in his spare time. When the story begins he is planning one that is to be his masterpiece.

Going round the city with Isaac as he delivers the watches he has mended, readers learn the history of the cathedral city in the Fens, going back to the days of the Normans. The huge cathedral that dominated the city frightened Isaac and he had never been inside it, but the fine Jaccomarchiadus clock for which it was famous, compelled him to go and see it from outside.

Another of Isaac's regular duties was to visit houses in the Close, including the Deanery, to wind the clocks, and that is how he comes to have his first terrifying meeting with the Dean. The ice is broken between these two contrasting people thanks to Isaac's error of putting someone else's watch paper in the Dean's watch case. These watch papers were little texts which Isaac had chosen as appropriate for the recipient, and the Dean's read:

> I labour here with all my might,
> To tell the time by day or night,
> In Thy devotion copy me
> And serve thy God as I serve Thee.

From this gentle, unspectacular start, the story continues to show how a strange assortment of people living in the city get caught up in events that revolve around the influence of the cathedral in their lives.

One of my favourite characters is Miss Montague, whose lovely Lyre clock is also wound regularly by Isaac. Apart from being a go-between for her friends the Dean and Isaac, she does not seem essential to the story, but in writing her in, Elizabeth gave such insight into all the facets of loving that Miss Montague's long life had revealed, that the book would have been much poorer without it.

'If anyone at this moment was thinking of her it was as a very old woman who never left her house … perhaps they pitied her. They did not know how vivid are the memories of the old and that only the young are house bound when they can't go out …

'Later she realised how much men and women owe to mere routine. She had for years led an extremely disciplined life, and now discipline held her up as irons hold the body of a paralytic.'

In the 1870s when the story is set, in the small city of Ely, it not only had a watchmaker's shop but an umbrella shop, with small, bulging windows, and a little umbrella made of tin and painted in stripes of red and blue, as a sign over the shop door. It was kept by the eighty-year-old Miss Bertha Throstle, to whom the Dean went for advice when wanting to purchase an umbrella for his small friend Bella.

The Dean felt Bertha summing him up pretty shrewdly. 'He on his side knew her to be sound as a nut', with the 'instinctive kindness of the good countrywoman.' For her part, Bertha 'was amazed that the Dean should be so feared in the city … Here was a rock! He made her feel as though she had firm ground under her feet. Hale and hearty though she was being eighty did at times make her feel a little insecure.'

The young characters in the book are just as sympathetically portrayed as the older ones—the young orphan chimney sweep Job Mooring whose fortunes take him from his cruel apprenticeship days with Albert Lee to working for Mr Peabody; his kind sweetheart Polly who could be happy with such small joys and thought that the stars sang. I can't help thinking that the sweet but wilful character of Bella, who ensnared the affections of the Dean, could only have been based on how Elizabeth remembered herself as a child.

The story ends with the death of the Dean on St Stephen's day, after using the text—'God is the Lord by whom we escape death'—when preaching the Christmas sermon the previous day, but his death brings reconciliation between all the people whose lives he has touched, and eventually causes Isaac Peabody to enter the cathedral, and regain his faith.

Writing about *The Dean's Watch*, Elizabeth explained that the man and woman she had remembered from the Gray's Inn ball were the inspiration for the Dean, Adam Ayscough, and his beautiful wife Elaine, but that in the interval between seeing them and writing the book, Adam 'had possessed himself of much of my father's character' while the beautiful woman had changed into the cold Elaine.

The preoccupation in the novel with the nature of spiritual love drew critical applause, but it was considered technically brilliant. After the Eliot Trilogy, it seems to be the book Elizabeth is associated with by the most people.

Although Elizabeth didn't drive, and by this time her health made long journeys too tiring, she was able to enjoy short drives with Jessie to the lovely countryside near them such as the Chiltern villages.

It's believed it was on one of these drives that Elizabeth caught a glimpse of an old house in one of the villages approached by a wonderful avenue of limes, which gave her the idea for her next novel, *The Scent of Water*, published by Hodder and Stoughton in 1963. Like *The Rosemary Tree*, she gave this story a modern (1950s) setting, using her gift for creating a story around simple things: lovely landscapes, children, the atmosphere of old houses, and beloved objects.

Paul, the blind poet and playwright in the story, reads from the Braille Bible his father has given him after he lost his sight: 'For there is hope of a tree, if it be cut down, that it will sprout again, and that the tender branch thereof will not cease. Though the root thereof wax old in the earth, and the stock thereof die in the ground; yet through the scent of water it will bud, and bring forth boughs like a plant.'

When Mary his companion has heard this, she asks, 'What is

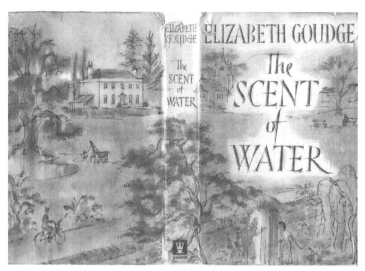

THE FIRST EDITION OF *THE SCENT OF WATER*
ALL SAINTS' CHURCH, PEPPARD

the scent of water?' Paul replies, 'Renewal. The goodness of God coming down like dew'. It is this renewal which comes to many of the people met within its pages that makes it an unusual, but highly satisfying book.

The collection of miniature treasures, 'The Little Things', which is left to Mary Lindsay by her aunt—'all so small that only the eyes of a child could fully perceive their glory'—is actually a description of a similar collection in a domed glass case that Elizabeth had been bequeathed by her Guernsey grandmother, and which she still possessed.

When writing the character of Mary Lindsay, who inherits 'The Laurels' from her cousin, I think Elizabeth was putting much of herself into Mary. This can be seen in several instances when she gives this reason for Mary having books by Jane Austen by her bedside: 'She liked her cheerful sanity. She had expected no great things of human nature, yet she loved it, and in Mr Knightley and Jane Bennet she had portrayed a quiet steady goodness that had been as lasting in literature as it would have been in life.' We know that Elizabeth took Jane Austen as a model for her own writing.

She writes of Mary's cousin's encounter with 'a queer old man' whose good advice stood her in good stead later in 'times of distress'; when trying to pray to her discarded God she quoted him: 'love, your God, is a trinity. There are three necessary prayers and they have three words each. They are these,

> Lord have mercy.
> Thee I adore.
> Into Thy hands.'

These words were later to be used at Elizabeth's funeral service and I am sure she must have been writing from a personal experience. She has Mary Lindsay reflect: 'For unbelief was easier than belief, much less demanding and subtly flattering because the agnostic felt himself to be intellectually superior to the believer. And then unbelief haunted by faith, as she knew by experience, produced a rather pleasant nostalgia, while belief haunted by doubt involved real suffering; that she knew now by intuition, soon probably she would know it by experience also.' In the realisation that her new life at 'Appleshaw' had brought her nearer, not only to her cousin, but to her dead fiancé, Mary recalls words from T.S. Eliot:

'And what the dead had no speech for, when living,
They can tell you, being dead: the communication
Of the dead is tongued with fire beyond the language of the living.'

This had been Elizabeth's experience too after the death of her parents. In *The Scent of Water*, as in her other writing, I am always impressed with her descriptions of the minor characters in her stories, which seems to show how well she understood ordinary people and the way their lives mattered in their community. Surely Mr and Mrs Baker were based on people she knew and appreciated. This is how Mary first met Mrs Baker, who had been looking after her cousin: 'Mary got to her feet and found herself confronting a little woman whose head scarcely reached her shoulder. Sparse grey hair was done up in an old-fashioned bun and very bright hazel eyes twinkled in a brown wrinkled face. She wore a clean apron over an electric blue skirt, and her hands were full of clean tea towels, her smile was wise and loving and there breathed from her whole person that sense of comfort and security, spiced with severity, that in the days of Mary's childhood had characterised the best nannies.'

She tells Mary about her husband, who though 'a bodger' by trade has 'obliged' in the garden setting the taties on Good Friday. Then Mr Baker, the bodger, comes to the door: 'He was as tall as his wife was tiny, and cadaverous as Don Quixote. He had ginger hair, a walrus moustache, a sad thin mouth and receding chin. He wore corduroy trousers tied below the knee with string and a strange duffel coat that hung so loosely from his gaunt shoulders that Mary was sure it had been bought at a jumble sale … There was a long pause and his Adam's apple began to work in his long thin throat. His voice, when it came, was that of a bronchitic corncrake.'

In Jean, the vicar's sister, we are again shown the real person behind the façade seen by most others, and the lovely old couple Mr and Mrs Adams present a truthful picture of the circumstances faced by many elderly couples: 'They had brought with them into her room the atmosphere of their own particular brand of courage … it was a delicate thing, the distillation of suffering that was never mentioned because courtesy forbade such a thing, and was not even interiorly dwelt upon.'

A description of Mary settling into her bedroom at 'The Laurels', possibly again reflects Elizabeth's life: 'She went upstairs again and in the last of the sunset light unpacked her things … stopping to look at the room and get the feel of it, for she was one of those women to whom the privacy of her bedroom is as important as his shell to a snail. It was always a matter of astonishment to her that those religious who slept not in cells but dormitories could retain their sanity.'

Set in the Chilterns, close to Elizabeth's home, the book gives glimpses of that lovely countryside, especially the beech woods so characteristic of it. Mr Baker's occupation as 'a bodger' was topical as since the 1700s the beech trees of the area have been a valuable commodity for chairmakers, with legs and spindles being made for furniture manufacture in High Wycombe.

There was not to be another novel from Elizabeth's pen until her last one, in 1970, *The Child from the Sea*. She was, however, kept busy compiling two poetry anthologies which will be looked at in the chapter on her religious writing.

In 1965 Hodder and Stoughton published a trilogy of her work under the title *Three Cities of Bells*, for which Elizabeth wrote this preface: 'This preface for a collection of three books about cathedral cities has given me an odd experience, for the first two books in this trilogy, written nearly thirty years ago and not looked at again until now, seemed to me when I took them from the bookshelf and turned their pages to have been written by a stranger. Anyone who has lived long enough to have been adult through the last thirty years, with all the changes they have brought and the central abyss of the war years slashed across them, knows this feeling when they re-read pre-war letters and diaries. They seem to belong to another age altogether, to have been written not by one's own friends and relatives but by strangers. Then a queer thing happens. Time telescopes or vanishes, and what is distant is not then but now. Reaching back into the past we have been like a kitten chasing its own elusive tail, and suddenly we catch the tail and are astonished to find it confronting us, a warm and living thing that appears to be part of ourselves.'

The children's books *Linnets and Valerians* and *I Saw Three Ships* are looked at elsewhere in the book.†

In the foreword to her last novel, *The Child from the Sea*, published in 1970, Elizabeth says it really began ten years earlier when she was staying at Jessie's holiday cottage in Pembrokeshire. There she had visited St David's Cathedral and afterwards was sitting on the cliffs above St Bride's Bay when she thought she saw a castle appearing through the mist. Later she was told she had seen Roch Castle where Lucy Walter, the mistress of Charles II, had been born.

This had already stirred up an idea for a book when she was lent a book written by one of Lucy's descendants, Lord George Scott, which claimed her character had been quite different to the popular

---

† *Linnets and Valerians* is looked at in the chapter 'Sudden Fame: Devon 1939–1951'. *I Saw Three Ships* is not covered elsewhere.

THE FIRST EDITION OF *THE CHILD FROM THE SEA*

version. Elizabeth said 'a carrot of that sort has to be pursued' and the book was used as the basis for her last novel.

Like *Green Dolphin Country* it is a very long book and takes its readers on a geographical journey. For although it begins at Roch Castle, it goes on to give a fascinating picture of London in 1640, with the story incorporating several historical characters from that period. Later, following the fortunes of Charles in exile, the story moves to Holland and France before culminating back in London after Charles is king.

This complicated but compelling book is a magnificent climax in the career of this gifted novelist. It is divided into three parts: The Child; The Idyll; The Woman, each part bringing a wealth of imagination and careful research to make it so believable. Elizabeth admitted there was very little to be found about Lucy Walter's childhood and that the first part of the book is largely fiction but that is difficult to credit as you read.

Lucy is eight years old when the story begins in 1638. Her father, William Walter, is said to be descended from Welsh princes and her mother from the Plantagenets. As well as two brothers, Richard and Justus, when the story opens the family also included Dewi and Betsi, twins sired by her father with a local girl, one of the things later causing the separation of her parents.

Lucy as a child is depicted as being a tomboy with a tempestuous but loving nature, with curly, unruly hair and unforgettable blue eyes. Through the account of her childhood we meet a variety of unusual and eccentric characters living at Roch: Parson Peregrine, a bachelor and scholar, who as well as tutoring the local boys keeps a pig called Ptolemy and hens named after the twelve tribes of Israel; also 'Old Parson' who keeps bees and who Lucy takes on a pilgrimage to St David's Cathedral to seek forgiveness for sins he cannot remember, but which are later to have a significant bearing on Lucy's life in later years. Nan-Nan, the diminutive Welsh woman, and John Shepherd the countryman, both of whom Lucy loves dearly, together with the frightening sin eater, give this first part of her childhood story, set on the beautiful Pembrokeshire coast where haunting cries of the seals could be heard, a magical introduction to a story that is to become poignant and tragic as the entanglements of Lucy's relationship with Charles are told.

The Civil War, which Elizabeth had shown in *The White Witch* had such impact on ordinary people everywhere, was also casting its shadow on this remote part of Wales as this passage warns: 'it was one of many such sparks all over the country, that would presently run together in a bitter conflagration, they refused to recognise, for the beginnings of tragedy, like the first warnings of pain, are always thrust out of sight; man's hope that what is pushed down into the dark will die there being as perennial as it is doomed.'

Lucy's first glimpse of Charles is when on a visit to London she waves to him as the royal barge passes under London Bridge. On the next, more private meeting, after exchanging their first kiss, Lucy gives Charles her pet marmoset. From this point Elizabeth explained that she adopted the Pembrokeshire legend that Charles and Lucy went through a marriage ceremony at the little church at Roch. It certainly makes a very presentable story, which restores the reputation of Lucy Walter in full measure. If there was ever any doubt of Elizabeth's incredible understanding of the complicated issues of love, this book must dispel it for ever. After Lucy and Charles returned from the boat trip where Charles had played a Hebridean lament on his flute to the seals, we find this passage: 'it deepened their union with each other in a way that belonged to the spirit alone; but each step nearer home brought them closer to their own mystery, the human mystery and predicament of loving so much that the condemnation of separateness laid upon human creatures becomes too great a burden ... the intensity of his sense of homecoming overwhelmed Charles. Here it was, the lost simplicity

… here was the deep well of water, and the fire and the bed of bracken beside it, and the girl who was his girl, and must belong to no one but himself alone … But he did not carry Lucy with him into its depth. Her childhood had not been the ceaselessly moving, over populated pageant that his had been and the few events that had struck hard upon her mind and heart had struck like a carver's chisel, and she acted now out of a simplicity of grief and loyalty unknown to him, and without premeditation. She twisted out of his arms and standing back with her hands behind her delivered her blows … in spite of his anger and desperate hurt he could almost have laughed; she was so resolved.'

So Lucy gives Charles his ultimatum: 'If you are gone I shall know I will never see you again. But if you are here I will know that I am to be your wife.'

This story ends with Charles's restoration to the monarchy when he has discarded Lucy, looks into the hearts of its characters and maybe gives a truer picture than the history books.

Elizabeth wrote of the book: 'it took years to write, and was beset by many interruptions that it became too long. I doubt if it is a good book, nevertheless I love it because its theme is forgiveness, the grace that seems to me divine above all others, and the most desperate need of all us tormented human beings, and also because I seemed to give it all I have to give; very little heaven knows. And so I know I can never write another novel, for I do not think there is anything else to say.'

This typically modest assessment of her work was not borne out, with the book becoming another best-seller throughout the world. It was, however, after nearly forty years of successful fiction writing, to be her last novel. For those readers who had been fortunate enough to read all her books, their feeling of sadness in knowing there would be no more delight flowing from her pen, must have been accompanied with gratitude for what her writing had brought to their lives, and the awareness that they had hopefully imbued some of her philosophy of life.

ELIZABETH AND JESSIE IN THE GARDEN AT ROSE COTTAGE

THESE THREE PHOTOGRAPHS APPEARED IN THE FIRST EDITION OF *WEG* ON ONE PAGE. I HAVE RESCANNED THE ONE ON THIS PAGE FROM *THE JOY OF THE SNOW* AND THE OTHERS COME INDIVIDUALLY FROM *WEG*.

INTERIOR OF ROSE COTTAGE

ROCH CASTLE, PEMBROKESHIRE

FOOTSTEPS IN
OXFORDSHIRE AND WALES

I first visited Rose Cottage and Peppard Common in June 1999. Jessie Monroe had continued to live in the cottage since Elizabeth's death, as in 1971 Elizabeth had put the cottage into joint ownership with Jessie. I had hoped to visit her there in the early spring of that year, but unfortunately she developed serious health problems and went into a nursing home in Wales, and my plans had to be put on hold.

By the summer Jessie was still not well enough to return to the cottage and decided the time had come to put it up for sale. On hearing this news I made hurried arrangements to go to see the cottage and garden while they remained as Elizabeth had known them.

Approaching the village on the road from Nettlebed, the Dog Inn was easily spotted, and then a short walk down Dog Lane brought me to Rose Cottage where an appointment had been made to show me round the empty cottage. In the lounge I tried visualising Elizabeth sitting by the old fireplace, as I'd seen in photographs, but it all seemed rather forlorn denuded of cosy furnishings and personal possessions that make a home.

The rather small, winding staircase leading to the bedrooms had a handrail to assist the climber, giving a poignant reminder of Elizabeth's arthritic problems even before the operations on her hip forced her to have a bed downstairs. Elizabeth's bedroom, heavily beamed like the rest of the cottage, had two small windows on either side of the room, with the rear one looking over the field where the white horse used to graze, and across to the view of the church spire.

It was a lovely summer's day, and out in the garden my spirits lifted, as thanks to the faithful gardener who was still caring for it, everywhere was as lovely as I'd imagined from Elizabeth's descriptions. It was easy to imagine the dogs racing round the grass between the variety of trees and shrubs. The herb garden, which Jessie made to copy the 17th-century one that Froniga would have used for her balms and potions, was flourishing; the scent of the old briar roses filled the air as we strolled round the garden. The well, which until fifty years ago would have been the only source of water for the cottage, stood close to the kitchen entrance, bringing the characters of Froniga and Yoben, created by Elizabeth in *The White Witch*, very much to mind.

My next visit to Peppard and the cottage wasn't until April 2001, when the new owners of Rose Cottage had kindly invited me to call. They were waiting for the builders to start on building an extension and make some necessary structural repairs, so once again I saw the cottage unchanged. The fact it was being lived in on this visit made it a happier one, especially as talking to them I felt the new owners were committed to preserving the essential character of the cottage. They were interested in hearing of the books Elizabeth had written using the local area and already had a copy of *The Joy of the Snow* showing the cottage on the front. Even on a damp day, following weeks of wet weather, the garden retained its charm, though the old apple tree had become rotten and had been felled. It was good to learn that their Westie dog will carry on the line of dogs playing in the garden.

On this second visit I had time to visit some of the people Elizabeth knew that were still living in the village, as well as the places she had used in her books. I called to see a courageous lady, Mrs Betty Harper, who had known Peppard all her life. She could remember when, as a child, she used to visit the old lady living then in Rose Cottage, sometimes sleeping in the same room as Elizabeth had done. She loved the old cottage so much she always wished she could live there, and after she had married she and her husband had a house built to look as similar to it as possible. Betty had left her job as a Land Girl during the war to come back to Peppard to help her ailing parents run the Dog Inn, later managing it with her mother. It was during this time she got to know Elizabeth, who would sometimes 'phone her when unexpected guests were arriving, asking Betty to take a bottle of sherry down to the cottage. She used to tell Elizabeth all she could remember about the history of the cottage and, like everyone else I met, Betty remembered her as a charming, gracious and very generous person, always ready to help local people who she heard were in need.

Betty told me of her friend Winnie's wonderful relationship with Elizabeth when she worked in the cottage for many years. The photograph I saw, and the description she gave of Winnie, seemed to suggest she was the inspiration for Mrs Baker in *The Scent of Water*, as also was her husband Alf, who helped in the garden, for Mr Baker. As an example of Elizabeth's generosity, Betty told how after Alf was no longer able to work, for fourteen years Elizabeth continued to pay his wages.

I was shown a little treasured tea set which had belonged to Winnie and which Winnie had formerly given to Elizabeth. When Winnie died, family problems meant her friends were not able to be given any mementoes, so Elizabeth passed the tea set to Betty, to have as a keepsake of her friend.

Betty told me how interested Elizabeth was when a pig farmer living further down the Pack and Prime lane won special prizes for his pigs, giving it as an example of how she related to people she thought of as genuine rather than to those who tried to cultivate her acquaintance because of her fame as a writer. She confirmed that the gypsies had for many generations used the field near Rose Cottage as a camp, moving around to other sites where seasonal work was available to them. She said they were real 'Romanies' as opposed to 'Travellers' and until a few years ago one of the gypsy women would always call when in the area—she understood they had now been given a permanent site where they were happily settled.

Another visit took me to meet Mrs Prosser and her daughter Pat, living across the road from the Dog Inn, in a house with the unusual name of Satsun, which I later learnt was because years ago Mrs Prosser and her late husband had built it themselves during their weekends.

Pat remembered how she and other children used to visit Elizabeth and how kind she was to them, talking about interesting things. They too have a treasured possession bequeathed to them by Elizabeth, a wall plate hanging in a place of honour. They had their own stories of Elizabeth's local generosity—of a boy she helped to pay to get through college, and many others. Mrs Prosser remembered how Elizabeth enjoyed hearing about the rough sea passage when she had gone to visit relatives in Guernsey and spoke of her own memories of the island.

During Elizabeth's last years, she offered to stay at the cottage when Jessie had to be away, as the paid carer didn't like being there alone. On these occasions Elizabeth insisted she had breakfast brought to her in bed by the carer. A happy memory was of the laughter they shared together, in spite of Elizabeth's health making her movements difficult. After Elizabeth's death Jessie unfortunately had a gas explosion in the kitchen of Rose Cottage necessitating considerable restoration, and for ten months she stayed with Mrs Prosser while the work was being done.

Like most places, Peppard Common has changed over the years since Elizabeth first moved there, and according to Mrs Prosser, what was once a tight-knit community now tends to be a sought-after area by affluent people, with several local places chosen for filming for TV productions.

The rector of Peppard church,† the Reverend Bob Butler-Smith, came there some years after Elizabeth and is soon to retire.†† He remembers taking communion to her at the cottage, although previously she attended the early Thursday communion service at the church. This rather ties up with what she wrote in her autobiography: 'I confess with shame that I have never enjoyed church services; unless taking place at Ely Cathedral, and then it was the cathedral that worked its alchemy upon the services and not the other way round. But there is an exception, a completely simple early morning communion service at any village church. At such a service one is not so much a complicated human being coming to a ritual that can be almost as complicated as oneself; one is that simple creature, the hart, coming to the water springs. And the place where they spring can become as beloved as one's home, and those who are with you there are no longer the congregation but the family.'

How brave and honest of Elizabeth to write this, and how it must have echoed the feelings of many, perhaps particularly those ex-clergy offspring like herself, who had their fill of complicated ritual, and now just longed for a simple relationship with God.

While I was in the locality Elizabeth had used in *The White Witch*, a visit to Henley was imperative. I imagine Elizabeth would have known Henley well during her more mobile years and, with her love of history, been well read about local involvement in the Civil War before she chose to write the book.

Henley remains a small, pleasant market town, with many old timbered houses and the famous riverside walks. There is a museum housing historical exhibits as well as ones connected with the rowing

† All Saints' Church.
†† Reverend Butler-Smith died in 2013.

activities that take place on the river. Being a Saturday when I visited, the information office which is sited within the Town Hall, was closed. Fortunately, helpful staff at the local library were able to find me some useful local reference books, including a booklet called *Henley and the Civil War*.

From it I learnt that Henley was not a good place to be in those times. The townspeople suffered at the hands of the Roundhead soldiers who were garrisoned there for a long time—houses were plundered, goods were seized without payment, and heavy taxes were levied upon the shopkeepers and traders.

It made it very clear that the inhabitants of Henley had no eagerness to fight, and loyalties were often decided by the influence of one man. In Henley this was a wealthy landowner, Sir Bulstrode Whitelocke, who ensured that the town was committed to supporting Parliament when the Civil War began.

I had found the character of Yoben, in his various guises, difficult to believe in, and doubted whether any such character could have existed other than in Elizabeth's imagination, but as I continued to read about Henley in the Civil War, I came upon information which made me change my mind: 'In November 1642, Rupert [the Royalist commander] had a Parliamentary spy, discovered in the town, hanged from an elm tree in Northfield End. The tree known as "Rupert's Elm" still stands by the roadside—everyone knows it.'

So there it was, Yoben's hanging, dramatically told in Elizabeth's story, tied up completely with this account, even to the season when it occurred.

In answer to my enquiries as to where to find the elm, the library staff told me that unfortunately, since the booklet was written, the tree had succumbed to elm disease, but the site could still be found quite near to the library.

Another incident from *The White Witch* was confirmed as historically accurate by the booklet: John Hampden's popularity in his home county (Buckinghamshire) enabled him to raise a regiment to support the Parliamentary cause on the outbreak of the Civil War. He dressed his men in a dark green uniform.

During the early months of the fighting, Hampden's troopers controlled the wooded Chilterns. It was they who were probably involved in the skirmish with the Royalists on the Mount outside Henley in late 1834 (see the chapter 'A fight in the streets'). But in 1643, Hampden was shot in a clash with Rupert's cavalry near the village of Chalgrove. He died from gangrene a week later. In *The White Witch* Elizabeth has Froniga, after she heard of the skirmish in Henley, refer to this as she prepared the remedies to take with her for the wounded: 'Never, as long as she lived, would she forget Colonel Hampden's unnecessary death ... Samile, milfoil and bugle ... She put them in her basket at once, together with remedies for shock and plenty of soft bandages.'

So it was clear that, although Elizabeth had altered the dates of some events to suit her story, the essential facts were historically based.

My efforts to find other local places mentioned in the story were not so successful, and I ended up concluding that Haslewood Manor and the little church where Parson Hawthyn and Francis found the gypsy children hiding behind a family monument were possibly an amalgamation of several places. By this stage of her career Elizabeth did this much more often than in her early days of writing. She wrote in her autobiography: 'We [novelists] give a story the setting of a place or countryside that we love but we are not accurate. Our memories go down into the subconscious, get overlaid with one thing and another and are fished up again anyhow and pieced together with the glue of sheer inventiveness ... We give the real place a fictitious name but that does not prevent it from being recognised ...' Being Elizabeth, she went on to say she was sorry to readers who had gone on a pilgrimage (as many did) and were irritated at not finding what they expected. Of course, there is no reason why she shouldn't mix places—she was writing fiction, not a travel guide—yet I must plead guilty to thinking I could be clever and find clues to the places she had in mind.

Geographically, I had considered the nearby Greys Court and church at Rotherfield Greys as possibilities for the manor and church mentioned in *The White Witch*. From Peppard, Rotherfield Greys can be reached either on foot down the Pack and Prime lane or a short distance by road from Peppard. The little church there does have some similarities to the one in the story, with its family monument of Sir Francis Knollys and his wife placed there in 1605. The list of rectors gives the name of John Hollin for the year of 1639, but six years later a new name appears—Robert Jones. So, like the fictional Parson Hawthyn, and many others like him, John Hollin was probably deposed during the troubles of that period. The estate of Greys Court was closed at the time of my visit because of the foot-and-mouth epidemic, so I wasn't able to see if there were any similarities with the fictional Haslewood Manor.

Sometime, by someone, I had been given the idea that the story of *The Scent of Water* had associations with the village of Turville, in the Chiltern Hills, so decided to explore that possibility next. To get to it from Peppard, the road takes you through the interesting village of Nettlebed, where in *The White Witch* Froniga takes Will to be cured of the 'King's Evil' by Charles I, who is there for a short visit. In *The Scent of Water*, as Mary heads towards Appleshaw to find 'The Laurels' which her cousin Mary has left her, and which she has not seen since a child, she remembers seeing an avenue of extraordinary trees before the village was reached and wonders if they are still there, or been replaced by a caravan site. The story tells us what she finds: 'She was within the avenue almost before she knew it, and the trees were the same. She stopped the car and got out and stood in the deserted lane looking up at them. If they were not quite as tremendous as she remembered, she had expected that … but even so they were immense and she felt their power just as she had as a child … Who had planted these giants in their ranks?'

I had mentioned this avenue of lime trees to several people in Peppard and had been assured I would still find them … We got out and stood in the deserted lane (except for two walkers laden with rucksacks), looking up at them. Although it was early spring and there was no sign of leaf, we could well believe the boy who had driven Mary and her father on their first visit there, when he said: 'Limes. Ain't another lime avenue like this in the country.'

Buoyed with the success of finding the lime avenue, I carried on into Turville, but here again I couldn't make the places match the story in most respects. For sure the beautifully kept church did have the requisite square tower, and the churchyard the slanting gravestones. I was surprised to find on a quiet early Friday afternoon several visitors inside the church until I was told the reason: it is the church that the TV comedy starring Dawn French, *The Vicar of Dibley*, used for the church shots.

Turville was a pretty little village to visit in spite of the torrents of water running down the street as a result of the unusually heavy rain. It is far enough off the beaten track to probably still provide the quality of life in the country that Mary appreciated in *The Scent of Water*. As this book is very similar to *The Rosemary Tree*, in as much that it does not matter a great deal to the story as to where it is set, I decided to 'call it a day' for my present 'footsteps' journey and carry away the memory of a part of the country still pleasant to visit as when Elizabeth enjoyed her drives there and was inspired to write another memorable book.

A holiday in Wales in September 1999 gave me the opportunity to visit Pembrokeshire and explore the places mentioned in the first part of *The Child from the Sea*. I went first to the small, remote city of St David's, on the tip of the south-west coast of Wales. Here in the 6th century, St David, the patron saint of Wales, established his church and monastery on the banks of the River Alun.

It is a most surprising place to visit, for although the cathedral gives it the status of a city, for over a thousand years it has remained almost a village. The present cathedral was started in the 11th century on the site of the old monastery, and was finished by the 14th century when a Bishop Gower also extended the existing Bishop's Palace, making a most magnificent building close to the cathedral. Both palace and cathedral were then enclosed within walls for protection from marauders from the nearby coast.

Another surprise, when coming to St David's, is to find the cathedral in a hollow, so that the approach is down quite steep steps, instead of up them as with many cathedrals. The Bishop's Palace was destroyed in the 16th century, but the ruins show just what an imposing building it must have been.

In *The Child from the Sea*, after listening to a fiery sermon given by Parson Peregrine on the subject of 'Pilgrimages', Lucy makes an impulsive decision that she will take 'Old Parson' on a pilgrimage to St David's so he can ask for forgiveness at St David's shrine. So, on a Sunday afternoon in August they set out on the ten-mile journey to St David's on Prince, her brother's horse, and Jeremiah, the kitchen pony. Their journey sounds delightful: 'Their pilgrim way led them first downhill to Newgale, where the sands fell away from the great pebble ridge that protected the cottages and the old inn from the Atlantic storms … Then uphill again to a great sweep of open country, thyme-scented in the heat, the turf cropped short by the grazing sheep. From here they could see Roch Castle on its rock, the Prescelly mountains remote and cloudlike to the east, and to the west the blue sweep of St Bride's Bay. The off-shore islands looked unearthly today, half-veiled in the heat mist, bird haunted and mysterious … Here and there one-storey white-washed cottages crouched behind thick ramparts of oaks and thorns blown almost horizontal, and then the way plunged downhill again into a deep valley, to the little port of Solva. Then up again and along the top, and almost before they knew it they were in the little city of St David's …'

After stabling their horses, and demanding to be brought buttermilk and bara ceirch to refresh them, Lucy leads Old Parson by the hand and they look down on 'the Valley of Roses—one of the places of power … its living strength could smite … with a perpetual shock of surprise … The walls and pinnacles and square tower of the Cathedral, honey-coloured in the sun and violet after rain, seemed always to live and breathe … The ruins of the bishop's palace beyond, delicate with long arcadings of empty arches against the sky.'

In the foreword to the book, Elizabeth apologised that she enables her pilgrims to meet the chancellor of St David's, Vicar Pritchard, by altering the time of his office there. Their time in the cathedral gives the two 'pilgrims' what Elizabeth calls a 'paradisal day' to always remember, as surely it must for everyone who visits this special place today. I followed Lucy's journey in reverse (but not on horseback), going from St David's to the village of Roch. I knew that Roch Castle, where Lucy Walter lived, was now in private hands and could not be viewed, except from the outside. Fortunately I had been lent an article written by the castle's owner, which gave quite a bit of information and had pictures of the interior, so, as I stood at the gate looking at the castle rising up from the rocks it was possible to imagine the young Lucy removing the iron bar from the narrow window in order to escape down to the sea and the caves where the seals have their breeding place.

In her novel, Elizabeth has the castle destroyed by the Civil War conflict before Charles comes to Roch to find Lucy again after their earlier tryst in Devonshire. I couldn't find any mention of any damage to it in the article about its history that I'd been given, which said that the castle had been built around 1250 by a Norman knight called Adam de Rupe—this name later changing to 'de la Roche', and finally anglicised to Roch.

It goes on to say that the castle was restored from a near-ruin just after the turn of the century c1900. Apparently, because the walls are six feet thick, the present owner (an American businessman) claims the interior spaces are small and few with the main door taking you to the guard room or barracks, where the men at arms must have cooked, eaten, and slept. By the time the Walter family lived there some of the original arrow slits would have been replaced with windows, and the tapestries and furnishings of the time would have made it a comfortable home by the standards of the time.

A few yards down the leafy lane from the castle I found the small church where Lucy and her brothers would have been baptised, and where Elizabeth decided the secret marriage between Lucy and Charles should take place in her book, although saying in the foreword to the book that according to legend it took place at Haverfordwest. Sadly, in common with many churches today, I found the church locked and contented myself with photographing it from the outside and rereading the account of it in *The Child from the Sea*.

In the short time since we had met Lucy and her family, the Civil War had brought a Puritan victory in Pembrokeshire, and Parson Peregrine had been told to conform to their beliefs in his church. On refusing, he had been made to suffer the consequences—his parsonage had been burnt down and he imprisoned. So it was his replacement, the Puritan Parson Gryg, that should have been asked to marry them, but Lucy would not hear of it, insisting that 'Old Parson' should do it, although he insisted they got Parson Gryg's consent. The age of consent then for a marriage was fourteen, so not a problem, but they had to arrange for the notary and his clerk from St David's to be present at the ceremony. It was these three men and her step-brother Dewi who were present in the little

THE PARISH CHURCH OF ST MARY, ROCH

THE LYCH GATE WITH THE INSCRIPTION 'HOLINESS UNTO THE LORD'

church, stripped bare of all its former 'popish trappings', when this early morning ceremony was said to have taken place. If walls could speak what would they tell, I thought, as I left the lonely little church guarding its secrets.

Another visit made possible by my stay in Wales was my longed-for meeting with Jessie Monroe. She had lived with Elizabeth for over thirty years and had known her better than anyone else. Jessie is now living at a residential home in a lovely house standing in large grounds in a beautiful area of Pembrokeshire.‡ She had always been a very active person and it was a difficult decision, after her illness, to decide the time had come to leave Rose Cottage and be looked after instead—she felt she would otherwise be causing anxiety to relatives and friends concerned for her welfare.

Jessie was looking very spry and well, sitting in her room with her walker at hand, when I went to see her. She seemed calm and content in spite of all that had befallen her during the last twelve months—her main sadness was being parted from her dog, who is now fourteen and was being cared for by another family.

Her memory was very good and we chatted for two hours about her time with Elizabeth from the time she first joined her in Devon. She said Elizabeth was then in a very poor state of health following her mother's death and her own illness. Jessie admitted that the first winter in Devon was so wet she felt she was never out of her waterboots, and the garden became flooded, making gardening impossible. She recalled scandalising visitors by telling them she hadn't read Elizabeth's books.

We talked about where Elizabeth did her writing—at one time they tried making a study from the old bakehouse or in a garden shed, but eventually had a board made to fit across her chair in the lounge where she could be most comfortable. Talking of *The Child*

‡ Jessie Monroe has since died.

from the Sea, Jessie said that she and her aunt who lived in Wales were able to help with much of the Welsh background needed for the book, and she emphasised just how hard Elizabeth worked when she researched for her books.

Talking about other places where Elizabeth had lived, Jessie said that although Elizabeth kept in touch with former friends there, she was never well enough to revisit any of them.

It was Jessie's opinion that Elizabeth took much more after her father than her mother, who in her opinion had been very demanding, expecting her meals 'on the dot', so that Elizabeth's writing had sometimes to be done early in the morning.

I asked Jessie about some of the people Elizabeth's books had been dedicated to as I hadn't been able to trace many, except the ones to the family and herself. The only one she was sure about was *The Child from the Sea*, dedicated to Freda Green, who was the wife of the clergyman at Marldon, but she added that other friends used to put themselves forward for this honour.

Talking about visitors, Jessie said that after her cousin Helene's early death, there weren't many relatives left, but the youngest 'Guernsey aunt' was still alive to visit at Rose Cottage, and Helene's two sons came there. Hugh was often there when training to be a Roman Catholic priest, and Mark's family came on day visits. There were, however, many devoted readers that wanted to visit, many from overseas, and Elizabeth would never turn anyone away.

I had noticed as we talked that a large portrait of Elizabeth hung on one wall, and when I mentioned something from one of the books that needed checking, Jessie directed me to a bookcase where she had all of Elizabeth's books. I think she has now made up for her early ignorance of them, as she advised me that every book needs to be read three times, first for the story, secondly for the descriptive background etc., and lastly for the real meaning and philosophy it contained.

She is right, of course, and although at the time it seemed rather a tall order, I've since attempted to follow that advice.

There wasn't nearly enough time to ask Jessie all I would have liked, but I was glad I had been able to talk to her and express my gratitude for all she did to help and support Elizabeth, enabling her to continue writing in spite of her many physical problems, and not least for creating the lovely garden which must have given her so much pleasure.

THE CREST OF THE WALTER(S) FAMILY, ON A GATE

RIGHT: THE MEMORIAL STONE FOR SOME OF LUCY WALTER'S DESCENDANTS

THE FAMILY NAME HAS BEEN SPELT WALTER AND WALTERS IN THE PAST, AS CAN BE SEEN HERE, BUT EG SPELLS IT WALTER IN HER NOVEL.

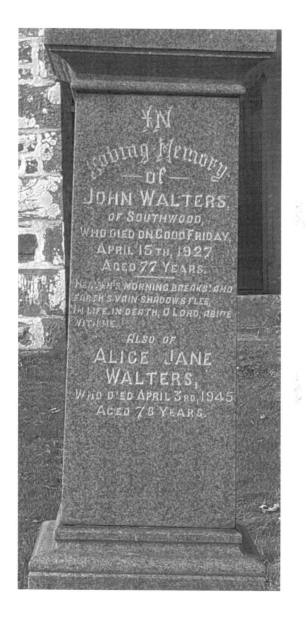

Elizabeth Goudge

THE JOY OF THE SNOW

An Autobiography

ANOTHER PICTURE OF ROSE COTTAGE ON A WRAPPER

THE RETIREMENT YEARS

1972–1984

Old age, I find, is a time when you start doing all the things that in earlier years you reprobated in older people, and were quite certain you would never do yourself.

Having told readers that *The Child from the Sea* would be her last novel, Elizabeth must have looked forward to having more time for the things she enjoyed—her house and garden, reading, and listening to her favourite music.

However, her friends and publisher were not prepared to let go lightly, and again urged her to consider writing her autobiography. Putting other people's interests first was second nature to her and she finally gave in, as she explained: 'Old age, I find, is a time when you start doing all the things that in earlier years you reprobated in older people, and were quite certain you would never do yourself, and if there was one thing more than another that I was determined not to do it was to write an autobiography. But the request that I should do so came from a few of those people to whom one can only say, in the words of Sir Philip Sidney, "Your desire to my heart is an absolute commandment." And so I obeyed.'

There is little doubt that Elizabeth was a compulsive writer and, 'having got her breath back' from writing her mammoth last novel, was probably more than ready to pick up her pen again.

She lets herself off her former resolved intention by saying that the book was hardly an autobiography, but an attempt to recapture happy memories, and share them with readers.

In any event, when *The Joy of the Snow* was published in 1974 it gave her readers a book worth waiting for, although Elizabeth had not found it easy, as an interview with Rosemary Marsh in the *Daily Telegraph* in 1972 shows: 'I have been filled with remorse and frustration. Looking back on past experiences from this new perspective can be quite harrowing. Yet I am glad I started writing like this, some of it is even self-indulgent; I like describing people I love.'

Rosemary Marsh breaks in here to say: 'Half way through the book finding the right phrase to express memories is becoming increasingly difficult for a tired author with an enormous following.' She then continued quoting Elizabeth: 'You can drive yourself physically and mentally, but can't force the creative faculty. The power gives out in a woman long before it does in a man. True, Agatha Christie is still just as productive, but there aren't many like her. [AC was ten years older than Elizabeth.] Sometimes I get so dissatisfied with my day's efforts that I wonder if the book will ever get published.'

Typically, as she wrote about past events, Elizabeth was judging herself: 'As I look back on my life I realise that together with the beauty of the world that holds them I have loved places too much and people not enough. Old age should enable us to redress, as far as possible, the imbalance of a life; in the case of earth lovers like myself, to detach ourselves as much as we can from the soil and wood and stone that will not endure, and live more deeply in eternal human beings.'

Even when she had finished writing the book, Elizabeth's life didn't get back to any semblance of normality for the rest of the summer. Writing to a friend in July, she said she had never been so busy in her whole life, with calls from newspapers and the BBC wanting to be given interviews prior to the publication of her book.

Once published, the already considerable volume of mail increased, which as usual she did her best to answer.

At the front of *The Joy of the Snow*, Elizabeth acknowledged the help two friends had given: 'Elsie Herron of Hodder and Stoughton who has edited this book for me, helped and encouraged and reassured me along the way, and to Kathleen Ault who for nearly forty years has typed my books, helped me with the proofs and grammar, and never failed to read my handwriting.' (What would writers give for such help today?) Kathleen Ault had been a typist for Canon Goudge, before undertaking to do Elizabeth's work as well. Having struggled with Elizabeth's handwriting myself, I think this recognition was well deserved, although Elizabeth apologised to friends that it had got worse over the years, and understandably so with the millions of words she had written by hand.

I hope and confidently expect that a large proportion of those reading this book will be fortunate enough to own their own precious copy of *The Joy of the Snow*, but knowing copies of the book are now difficult to obtain, I've concluded it is expedient to give a summary of it in order to give an idea of the scope and contents of the book, as well as my use of it in writing *The World of Elizabeth Goudge*.

The book begins with a quotation from Ben Jonson, which Elizabeth compared to the opening of 'a happy nunc dimittis'; 'Have you seen, felt, smelt, tasted the beauty of the world?'

Answering this she said: 'I am one of the fortunate, for I have never lived in a place that was not beautiful', and she went on to tell of her happy childhood in Wells, giving a fascinating account of that small city at the beginning of the 20th century.

In a chapter entitled 'Story Telling', Elizabeth tried to address questions on the craft of writing which readers had asked over the years. She compared it with other activities such as carpentry, embroidery or even having a baby, which she considered needed love, imagination and physical labour, as much as writing.

She also paid tribute to her readers: 'I owe my readers an incalculable debt, which I shall never be able to pay. I am not only grateful that they need me at all, I am even more grateful for the affection which for forty years they have expressed in so many delightful ways. From among them have come some of my greatest friends.'

In the chapter called 'The Island', Elizabeth told of her summer visits to her maternal grandparents in Guernsey. The island, now so popular with holidaymakers, was then quite remote from the rest of the world, and had been even more so during her mother's childhood, which she also recalled.

This chapter shows how much in her character and gift of imagination was inherited from this side of her family. This is one description of them that she gave: 'The Channel Islanders are a proud people, and my mother's family were no exception to the rule. One of my aunts once said to me, "We think a lot of ourselves" and indeed they did. They claimed that the founder of the family was William the Conqueror's cupbearer, who fought in the Battle of Hastings.' Her account of life in pre-First World War Guernsey not only tells us of her family's background, but also gives much of the island's social history as well.

If 'The Island' showed the influence on her of her mother's family, another chapter called 'The Family of the Silk Weaver' explains the very different one given through her father's family. Here is how Elizabeth tells about them: 'The first ancestor of whom I have any knowledge is William Goouds, a Flemish Huguenot weaver whose family came to England and settled in London. He established himself in business and did well, becoming a flourishing silk merchant, and was admitted to the Freedom of the City of London and Worshipful Company of Weavers.'

I wonder if Elizabeth knew about him when she set up her loom at Ely?

Of her paternal grandfather she wrote: 'He spent his days going backwards and forwards to the Bank of England, and cultivating his garden in his free time.' The family had apparently adhered to the Protestant Evangelical opinions of the Huguenot forebears, and her father's strict upbringing could not have been in greater contrast to that of her mother's carefree childhood.

It seems that Henry Goudge took more after his mother, as Elizabeth said his brilliant mind closed down altogether when it came to business and 'he was scarcely able to ascertain if the right change had been given him when he bought a railway ticket'.

Elizabeth Bennet, the grandmother Elizabeth was named after, was 'very delicate and through almost the whole of her children's memory, suffered from asthma, and from the melancholia that is the skeleton in the family cupboard'.

There seems little doubt that Elizabeth was including herself as well as her father here, as later in the book when she describes how 'after a period of strain or overwork darkness could fall upon him [her father] suddenly, out of the blue and last for weeks', she understood, as it was similar to 'her demon who brought darkness' and was determined she should not write books. Fortunately, after the move to Rose Cottage Elizabeth felt she had been released from her demon for good.

Reading about the Goudge side of her family it becomes clear that many of the traits she inherited from them (apart from the melancholia), were ones that served her well during her rewarding, but not always easy, life—courage, hard work, perseverance and a humble love of God and man, amongst others.

Before going on to her life at Ely, Elizabeth included a chapter called 'The Edwardians', which, while giving more glimpses of her family's life, also gives a fascinating insight into what living then, without many of today's conveniences, would have been like. Here is one of them: 'Washing long hair at home was quite an undertaking and so was washing bodies without the aid of bathrooms. There were large marble topped washstands in each bedroom with patterned jugs and basins ... Our home possessed bathtubs of two sorts, some round, some shaped like armchairs and these were placed in the bedrooms at night with an early Christian beside it. These early Christians were a fascination to a child. I do not remember how they got their name. It was not a name known to the trade I'm sure. Probably my mother invented it because they were meant to encourage early rising. They were small brown wicker hampers, tubular shaped, lined with cotton wool and twill of a vivid shade of scarlet. At bedtime metal containers filled with hot water were put inside and they were carried upstairs one by one and placed in each bedroom beside the tub. I imagine you did what you liked with it, using the hot water there and then or keeping it until the morning when it would still be hot and could be used for shaving as well as washing ... Children and servants were the lucky ones. Children bathed in a tub before the day-nursery fire and the servants bathed beside the blessed warmth of the kitchen range.'

Elizabeth was only eleven years old when her family moved from Wells to Ely, so when writing the autobiography she was looking back sixty-odd years. Yet she was able to describe the city, cathedral, and her life as though it had been yesterday.

Looking back can give pleasure, but can also cause dismay, knowing that some things have not changed for the better. Elizabeth realised this when remembering the cowslips she had enjoyed seeing at Ely: 'In the shade of these trees [wild crab apple] bordering the way grew enormous cowslips. There was much waste ground in the fen in those days and whole fields would be cloth of gold from hedge to hedge. In D. H. Lawrence's *Sons and Lovers* there is a description of just such a field, a description so perfect that when I read it I could have wept; for sheer joy at the marvel of the poet's writing and also for sorrow, for the Ely cowslip fields and the droves that do not exist any more. The old ways still link the farms, it is true, but they are macadamised and the trees have been cut down. It is right that there should be no more waste land but could there not be a cowslip sanctuary somewhere? A patch of them preserved as fritillaries are preserved in Magdalen Meadows at Oxford; to show a later generation what fields looked like once upon a time.'

I share the same feeling with the disappearance of similar fields where I grew up. Elizabeth was not a sentimentalist who wanted nothing to change, and would have been the first to approve the improvements that have replaced the poverty and bad housing in Ely that existed at that time.

The subject of the next chapter in her book, ESP, a popular one when she was writing, has now been revamped with 'New Age labels'; nevertheless it is an interesting chapter that deals candidly with Elizabeth's own experiences of ghosts, spirits and telepathy, and the explanations for some she has arrived at. The years spent in Devon as well as her Guernsey ancestry made her take these topics on board naturally.

The chapter called 'Non-Education' is rather a misnomer because it deals with her time at a boarding school in Hampshire and the two years spent at Reading School of Art. It is really Elizabeth putting herself down (which she was always good at), because she didn't acquire any academic qualifications to equip her to earn her own living. She wrote: 'What to do with me was a problem for my poor parents once they had grasped the fact that their daughter knew next to nothing ... academically speaking there was no hope for me ... parents of that era realised that unless their daughters had exceptional beauty and charm they would not marry. The First World War left few young men alive ... and so at that time there were millions more women than men in England.'

She recalled the situation when for the first time women were liberated and a large and varied field of work was opening to them.

213

She reflects how she came to terms with the way this had affected her life: 'I am one of the many who have found great joy in work and in building up a career. I have even lived to "Thank God fasting for the single state." Though you have to be fairly old before you can recognise and deeply prize the blessings of a single life, for up to that point the deprivation of childlessness is hard to bear.'

Elizabeth had a very loving nature and made no secret to her friends that she would like to have married and had children, though acknowledging she would not have had the same opportunity to write had that happened. Happily, she had come to realise that there was nothing to prevent a single woman experiencing the richness of falling in love now and again in her life. Being open to love was probably the secret of her charm.

The two chapters she wrote about life at Oxford and Barton, spanned seventeen years and saw the blossoming of her writing career, and of opportunities to travel which provided more ideas for her stories.

Before writing two chapters about the years spent living with her mother in Devon called 'The Ark' and 'Westerland', she wrote one called 'Pain and the Love of God', in which she tried to share some of the conclusions she had reached on this baffling question, and one that she had probably been asked about in letters from her readers. As well as witnessing the pain of those she loved, Elizabeth had also had her own share of mental and physical pain, so she could write from experience.

In a chapter called 'To Make an End is to Make a Beginning', she tells about her mother's last illness and the move to the home where she was to live for the next thirty years—Rose Cottage in Oxfordshire. This is how she explained her decision to write it: 'When I started this book I told myself that in writing it I wanted to think only of the happy memories unless a dark period should lead out into some new and happy knowledge.' By writing of her mother's last illness she hoped to show others what she had found, that what sometimes appears to be useless, pointless suffering can prove to be the last stage of purification leading to a peaceful end.

Following her mother's death and her last visit to Hampshire, on her return to Devon she attempted to get back into her routine of writing but found it a struggle. This is when an understanding friend gave her the advice to contact Jessie Monroe as a possible companion.

We have already seen how this worked out very happily and led to living at Rose Cottage. In a chapter called 'Gratitude', Elizabeth acknowledged that the basic things like temperament inheritance, upbringing and early experience cannot be changed, but concluded that everyone's seeking and struggling can be influenced by the people met and lived with, books read etc., which help create an everlasting and changing personality.

She then went on to look back at all the people and events in her own life which had resulted in the writing of each of her books, and she told which ones she herself liked best and why.

In the book's final chapter, 'The End of our Exploring', as the title suggests, Elizabeth drew together the conclusions she had reached about her beliefs and the essential power of love, ending with a verse by Thomas Traherne: 'O God, who by love alone art great and glorious, that art present and livest with us by love alone; Grant us likewise by love to attain another self, by love to live in others, and by love to come to our glory, to see and accompany Thy love throughout eternity.'

Elizabeth's reputation ensured that her autobiography created considerable interest, and articles about the book and its author appeared in *The Times*, *The Sunday Times* and *The Church Times*, after its publication in August 1974. They all re-traced her life and the success her books had achieved. They paid tribute to her qualities of humility and compassion, and mentioned the gift of happiness she acknowledged had been given by her parents, and the freedom that old age was bringing.

The autobiography was virtually Elizabeth's swansong, even though two years later she wrote a foreword to *A Book of Faith*. Her writing during the next ten years was chiefly letters to friends at home and abroad. It is thanks to some of these friends who valued and kept her letters that I have been able to get some idea of how she spent those years.

Being always, by her own acknowledgement, a shy and reticent person, Elizabeth did not make friends lightly, but her letters show that once a friendship had been established she valued and appreciated it.

Madeau Stewart was a broadcaster, musician, and writer who became a friend of Elizabeth's in the early 1970s. She worked for the BBC in their sounds archives and later as a producer for Radio 3 programmes. Although Elizabeth may have known of her earlier in connection with her work, the friendship seems to have been sealed after Madeau interviewed Elizabeth at Rose Cottage for a programme being made about her.

The friendship, chiefly maintained by correspondence, plus occasional visits by Madeau, seems to have been based on their mutual interests of music and love of the natural world. Elizabeth first mentioned this in her foreword to *The Child from the Sea*, when she wrote: 'I would like to express my gratitude for a talk I heard years ago on the BBC. It was for Welsh schools and was given by Madeau Stewart. She described how she played her flute to the seals.'

From the correspondence it would seem that they also shared a similar outlook on many matters.

When the correspondence first began Madeau was living in Sussex, but on her retirement in 1978 she moved to a cottage near Burford, where Jessie was able to visit her on the way back from a holiday and tell Elizabeth about it.

Because of Madeau's respect for Elizabeth's work, and her realisation of their possible future interest, she arranged for Elizabeth's letters to be deposited at the Oxford Record Office.

Elizabeth's writing had always been very popular in the USA and readers from there would not only write to her, but on visits to England would 'go on pilgrimages' to the places they had read about in her books. Elizabeth recognised the sincerity, and warmth of feeling of these fans—ever since an American sailor had walked from his base at Dartmouth in Devon in order to express his pleasure at her MGM Award, she had retained a soft spot for his countrymen.

So, quite often Elizabeth would receive requests from these fans to be allowed to call on her, and whenever possible she would welcome them to Rose Cottage. Amongst these there were some who became long-term friends and corresponded with her afterwards. Like Madeau Stewart they valued and kept her letters to them, and I have been fortunate enough, thanks to a kind mutual friend, to have three of these share with me what Elizabeth wrote to them about during the last years of her life.

One of these American friends, a Doctor of Philosophy, first wrote to Elizabeth in 1954 whilst serving in the US Navy on Guam Island. He had read her books and, having a keen interest in literature, wanted to send his appreciation of them—he received a prompt reply to his letter, thanking him for his encouragement.

After leaving the navy, he opted for a career teaching philosophy, continuing to read her new books as they were published. When planning his first visit to the UK for 1972, he wrote again to Elizabeth, telling her of his continued interest in her writing and of his present career, chosen in preference to a literary one. Her reply is interesting: 'Trying to earn a living by writing can (only at times) almost make one hate the sight of a book.'

He mentioned their holiday (in May) was to include a visit to Scotland, to which Elizabeth replied: 'You are going to the most beautiful part of it, and at a time of year (so they say in Skye) that it stops raining for a while.'

The letter also suggested suitable dates at the end of May when she would like them to visit her. The next letter in late August of that year indicates the visit took place before their tour continued to Oxford, Ely and Wells. After another visit in 1974, the correspondence continued regularly with Elizabeth taking much interest in his teaching work, saying in one letter: 'I think all who teach are just about the most important people in the world just now, for they are with the young and can help them as no one else can do.'

Like all those fortunate people to have met Elizabeth, this man remembers her as one of the kindest people he has ever met, generous with her time and concerned for the welfare of others. She and her writing have had a considerable influence on his life.

This feeling is echoed by another American visitor, who after being enthralled by reading *The Child from the Sea*, sent Elizabeth a painting depicting a scene in the book. This led to a correspondence and, in 1973, to an invitation to visit Elizabeth at Rose Cottage. She has vivid memories of her visit there with her husband and daughter, and of being shown a small glass-fronted cupboard which contained 'The Little Things' mentioned in *The Scent of Water*.

She remembers them being given 'cookies' called Angel's Trumpets with their tea and of Elizabeth giving her a sprig of rosemary from the bush in the garden.

She too wrote to and received letters from Elizabeth, and believes that meeting Elizabeth and reading her books have inspired so much of what she does and how she lives. It is her opinion that 'the threads that EG so often wove throughout her books connecting people to people, are still vigorous and doing their work'. Recalling how often, while doing my research, I was given unexpected new leads, I'm inclined to agree with this theory.

Although the osteoarthritis was making her mobility increasingly

218

difficult, for the first few years of her retirement, Elizabeth was able to continue enjoying her favourite activities.

Her letters show clearly that she enjoyed the garden, with frequent mentions of the flowers in bloom at the time of writing. When arranging dates for friends to visit she would explain that Wednesdays were sacrosanct as her gardener's day.

Although not a musician (since playing the violin at school), she considerably enjoyed listening to music. One friend who stayed at the cottage remembers being asked to play the piano, and how on one visit a new radiogram had been bought and how the better quality it gave to their listening was much appreciated.

Elizabeth often spoke to Madeau of music she had enjoyed in her programmes, and wrote in one letter: 'Sometimes I think music is our only hope. Evil can't get hold of it. It is entirely spiritual and is truly the voice of God. Musicians are more important in days like these than writers.'

Reading had always been another constant source of pleasure, and the bookcases at the cottage were always well stocked. Her love of Shakespeare and poetry made the compiling of three poetry anthologies a pleasant task. How much she knew and read of her contemporary writers is not clear, but in a letter to Madeau she mentioned that she sometimes met Ruth Pitter, who lives in the Chilterns, calling her 'that dear and funny poet'.

The importance of the influence of books in her life is something she frequently stated. Writing to the Doctor of Philosophy about his students' study of the writing of C. S. Lewis, Elizabeth said: 'I owe more to his books than I can possibly say.'

Although travelling was now confined to short car journeys, travel books were often ones she enjoyed, as were radio and TV programmes on that subject.

The death of her cousin, Helene, in the early 1960s had been a big sorrow, but she continued to enjoy visits from Helene's two sons (also her godsons)—Mark with his wife and family, and Hugh, who often stayed while training to be a priest in the Roman Catholic Church. Later on she attended Hugh's ordination, having bought him his chalice and breviary in lieu of his mother. When Hugh went out as a priest to Peru, Elizabeth corresponded with him regularly and often included news of him in letters to her friends. Like her father, Elizabeth was very ecumenical in her outlook and would have taken keen interest in Hugh's work.

Irene was the last of the Guernsey aunts left to visit her at Rose Cottage, but there remained one other link with that side of her family—a second cousin (their grandmothers were sisters) now lived at West Challow near Wantage. Sibyl Hatton was three years older than Elizabeth and on Elizabeth's occasional visits to her they must have enjoyed sharing their memories of their family and of Guernsey. A mention of Sibyl in a letter to Madeau illustrates Elizabeth's quiet sense of humour: 'When Sibyl lost her husband (who was Dean of Wells) John Betjeman gave her a gift for her comfort (typical of him I should think) of a disused coalyard. It had been a perfect site for a little home. She has put up a little bungalow with a garden round it. The flowers come up with soot on their faces.'

Although at the beginning of her years at Rose Cottage Elizabeth was homesick for Devon, she grew to love living in the old cottage, saying that quietness was helped by living in a house that was very old, and that all old houses have the serenity and acquiescence that old age should bring.

All who visited Rose Cottage attest to the warmth of welcome they received. In her autobiography Elizabeth insists it was the benign influence of the cottage that was responsible: 'The great and Christian virtue of hospitality is a rather weakly plant in myself and Jessie; it needs a lot of nurturing, but in the cottage itself it is so strong that the moment the front door is opened to a guest I can feel the delight that rises from its hospitable old heart. I once entertained thirty writers in our sitting room and even above the noise of the thirty talking at once I imagined I was aware of the contented cat-like purring of the cottage. It liked it. This cottage knows in its wisdom how much human beings need each other.'

The three successive Dandie Dinmont dogs that shared the cottage and garden with them were another source of pleasure, although their short span of life, which Elizabeth said only averaged ten years, meant a fairly frequent sad parting. However, like many other dog owners, getting to know and love one breed in particular made them choose the same one again the next time around. Even then, they found that each dog had its own very individual personality. In the early sixties, after the death of Tiki, they chose one they called Randa (short for Miranda) who was completely the opposite, preferring to be indoors and disliking to even get her feet wet.

At the time Elizabeth was writing her autobiography, Randa had been succeeded by another Dandie Dinmont dog called Froda, who enjoyed making herself a bower in a clump of honeysuckle in the garden. Froda was then only three and Elizabeth wrote that she hoped Froda would outlive her, but in a letter to Madeau in June 1978 she writes that Froda had died and that this time they have chosen a different breed, a Shih-Tzu called Tasha, from a rescue home. She doesn't give Tasha's age and sadly that dog also died a very short time before Elizabeth's death.

When writing about the death of Max, their pre-war dog, Elizabeth said: 'Believing as I do (and I have no less a person than C. S. Lewis to back me up) that the love we have for our animals insures their immortality for as long as the love lasts …'

Writing to Madeau just after the death of Froda, Elizabeth told her: 'I asked a friend of mine in the next world to look after Froda and she did—showing me one morning B. and F. together in their ethereal bodies (Jessie naturally rather sceptical of my early morning visions).'

In the photographs that accompanied articles at the time of the publication of *The Joy of the Snow*, it is Froda who is pictured with Elizabeth sitting in the comfortable chintzy room by the old open fireplace. Apparently some of the overseas visitors to the cottage were somewhat surprised at the simplicity of Elizabeth's lifestyle, but she had long ago said she had no wish to live as a rich woman, and was quite content with her peaceful home containing mementoes from the past, like the tapestry screen made by her great-grandmother in Guernsey in 1809. There were horse brasses decorating the old beams which Jessie had bought her, a different one each time a book was published.

Whether naturally tidy, or trained to be so by her nanny from her early years, everything indicates that Elizabeth liked to have things kept orderly. She told a reporter visiting her that Jessie was a great help in this as in all ways: 'she sorts out my papers, tidies, checks my files, and ruthlessly throws away all superfluous material.'

It was on Elizabeth's instructions that towards the end of her life, Jessie was told to burn all the papers connected with her writing life. Some of the reason I'm sure was her thought for others who might have to spend time doing it when she was gone and also her modest conviction that the papers would be of no lasting interest to anyone else.

By 1977, Elizabeth's letters began to give an indication of the health problems which from then on were to plague her last years. Her blood pressure was found to be high, coupled with the hardening of the arteries. This, with the already trying osteoarthritis, understandably made her rather depressed, and writing to Madeau she said: 'health is so important for happiness—I suppose it ought not to be, but it is.'

Another frustration which Jessie told me of was that from time to time Elizabeth would make an attempt at writing again (perhaps another children's book she had said she might like to do). However, her poor concentration meant she had to give up on it.

There was no mention of this in her letters and she continued to take an interest in all that her friends did. She occasionally mentioned changes happening in Peppard and the outside world which she did not find to her liking—trees had been cut down in the lane and motor cyclists even were sometimes heard riding there. There was a possibility of building right opposite the cottage, but this fortunately didn't happen. She said that she and Jessie would half-heartedly look for a bungalow, as the garden was getting too much for them, but added that at the bottom of their hearts they didn't want to leave Rose Cottage.

Then in the early spring of 1978 Elizabeth had a fall in the house and had to be admitted to hospital. Despite Jessie's misgivings, Elizabeth chose to go into a public ward at Reading hospital.

In retrospect, knowing her love of privacy, it seems an odd decision and certainly wouldn't have been for financial reasons. Possibly, because she hadn't been in hospital as a patient for some time, her awareness of the changes wrought by the NHS was limited. Or it may have been her socialist leanings, wanting to be part of ordinary people's lives, that influenced her decision.

Whatever the reason, Elizabeth's stay in hospital was to prove that she had not lost the ability to observe and empathise with the pain and distress of others, as the poem she wrote about the experience, 'Easter in the Ward', shows. It not only conjures up a very accurate picture for those who were also in hospital about that time, but shows the essence of her faith.*

The injured leg continued to be a problem, as seven months later in November Elizabeth wrote to Madeau: 'I should be able to go upstairs again when the bone knits. There is much pain with

* See page 226.

the pin pressing on a nerve in my leg. The pin should come out by the end of January.'

From now on Elizabeth jokingly referred to 'Edward, my naughty leg', trying to make light of what was still a problem. In June and July Elizabeth wrote twice to Madeau from St Luke's Home, Oxford, where she was being looked after while Jessie went on a much-needed break to Wales. In the first of those letters she said she was due to go back to Reading hospital to see the consultant and have more X-rays. In the second letter she reported she was walking on sticks which she had to learn to manage before returning home.

Further operations proved necessary with long stays in hospital—for three months the leg was in traction. The setback made Elizabeth consider whether she ought to go into a nursing home permanently, but she told Madeau that Jessie wouldn't hear of it, and the little room downstairs was to be made into a bedroom for her.

Letters to friends in 1981 suggest a relatively calm period during which she attempted to 'put her affairs in order' and ran into trying complications over tax matters. One highlight of the year was a visit by Madeau and her cousin Rosemary.

1982 did not begin well, with Elizabeth having another fall in January which meant another stay in hospital. In treating the broken femur it was discovered that her back bone was crumbling, making the placing of a pin very difficult. Back home again she replied to the concerns of friends about her health, saying: 'I am like King Charles 2nd, I am being an unconsciously long time dying.' She went on to say how grateful she was, that, thanks to Jessie, she was still in her own home.

Ten years on from the publication of her last novel, Elizabeth's books were still so popular that new editions were being printed, often in paperback form. The BBC contacted Elizabeth about the possibility of making a TV programme about her life, but the idea had to be abandoned because of her poor health. Elizabeth had always been a listener to *Desert Island Discs*, and confided once to a friend that she would have liked to have been asked onto the programme, but her mobility problems in getting to a studio didn't make that possible either. Not having been fortunate enough to meet her, I feel very sad that neither of those recordings was made for posterity.

I did contact the BBC to see if her earlier broadcast was available, but the answer was negative.

In 1983 another trial was added for Elizabeth to endure—cataracts were affecting her sight, making reading and writing difficult. Again typically, Elizabeth's thoughts were that her friends shouldn't think she had forgotten them by not writing, and a printed letter was sent, explaining the situation: 'Dear ... Thank you very much for your kind letter. I am sorry that owing to illness and failing sight, I can no longer answer letters.'

Over recent years her friends had told her they were praying for her, and I'm sure she continued to keep them in her thoughts, even though she no longer wrote to them.

A final letter to Madeau Stewart, dated March 25th, 1984, written by Jessie, but signed by Elizabeth, told of another fall and stay in hospital. Although back in her beloved Rose Cottage, she never really recovered and died there peacefully on April 1st a few weeks before her eighty-fourth birthday.

Obituaries were published locally and nationally. *The Times* newspaper ended its tribute with these words: 'Fragile in appearance, but strong in spirit, she seemed at one with the peace and simplicity of her setting. Few novelists have had comparable knowledge and faith in the goodness of human nature, the beauty of childhood, and the pursuit of things lovely and of good report. As with Jane Austen, she "let other pens dwell on guilt and misery".'

A service of thanksgiving was held at Peppard church on Friday,

April 6th at 2.30 p.m. At Elizabeth's request, any donations in lieu of flowers were to be given to 'The Invalid Children's Association'.

During the service, attended by her family and friends, Thomas Traherne's prayer with which she had ended her autobiography was said. Also the words she had quoted in *The Scent of Water*—

> Lord have mercy.
> Thee I adore.
> Into Thy hands.

So Elizabeth set out on her last journey freed from pain and the disablement of the last years, leaving behind a unique record of a writer's spiritual pilgrimage and awareness of things unseen but eternal.

Easter in the Ward

Tomorrow it would be Easter Day.
Beyond the high hospital windows
There must be a freshness in the world;
Trees unfurling their dear April green,
The doves calling, kingcups by the stream,
White violets scenting the hedgerows.

The windows showed only stark chimneys.
The hot and crowded ward held much pain,
Many uncomforted tragedies.
Day and night they came in, lying still
On the stretchers, shocked and much afraid.
Cars and lorries passed but no birds sang.

If only they could be comforted!

The gypsy girl, battered by hard blows,
Struggling out of her bed to run away.
'Lie still, dear,' we would say. 'You are safe.
Lie down again.' But she could not rest.
She must run from the blows and escape.

And another girl, comely and brave.
Her boy's motor cycle, wildly swerving
Had crashed them both against a lorry
Would she walk again? No one could know.
Broken limbs strung up on traction
She laughed and was sure she would get well.

Not all sadness. By day there were joys.
Sister competent, serenely kind.
Young nurses, mostly kind, sometimes not,
But good to look at, full of laughter.
Pots of bright flowers, shafts of sunlight,
Small children visiting Mum or Gran.

But there seemed no comfort for the old:
So old myself, how I ached for them.
'You do not know what I have suffered'
Said one. She was right. Pain is private.
'What would my poor husband say if he
Could see me now?' another asked me.

They all feared the geriatric ward
As once old people feared the workhouse,
A place from which you never come out.
I was ashamed, safe home behind me.
I prayed. 'Christ, have mercy on the old.'

Why was he not here to comfort them?

Ours is now, they say, a heathen land.
The ward had not noticed Good Friday.
Would we remember Easter morning?
'We used to,' said a nurse I had asked.
'We used to sing hymns in the chapel.
Lovely, it was, we don't do it now.'

She spoke sadly, for she was sorry.
If only he would come tomorrow,
Despite our ignoring of his cross,
Walk down the ward in the living light
Of resurrection glory, what then?
There would be none left uncomforted.

I could not sleep that night, wanting him.
The ward was strangely quiet, peaceful
As it seldom was. No accidents,
No distress, moaning or restlessness.
Yet I felt no peace and prayed to die,
Less I should burden those who loved me.

A clock struck. Midnight. A new day born.
Easter morning and I prayed for death.
'To die into your resurrection.'
Could one ask for any greater gift?
I asked for it again and again.
'To die into your resurrection.'

The hours passed and there was no answer.

Dawn came and with it a line of verse.
'The shining silence of the scorn of God.'
But the poet was mistaken there,
Our courteous Lord was never scornful
And silence can be love's still small voice,

Asking that we should wait a moment,
Accepting from him the proffered gift
Of his own everlasting patience …
Yes, but for us his divine moments
Seem an eternity of waiting.
When, merciful love? When will you come?

Full dawn now. What was that joyous noise?
Trumpets of the dawn? Easter trumpets?
No, a dear familiar clattering,
A musical clinking and ringing.
Heads lifted from hot pillows. There was
Hope and expectation in the ward.

It was Ida with the tea trolley,
Dear black Ida, rattling and banging,
Swaying and singing down the long ward.
Like a ship in full sail was Ida,
Crying aloud the tidings of joy.
'Cup of tea with sugar? With sugar?'

Her proportions were large as her heart,
Her eyes and teeth flashed in her dark face
As she flung back her head in laughter,
Singing, most days, snatches of old songs
Interwoven with that joyous cry,

'Cup of tea with sugar? Sugar?'

Her singing voice, deep and glorious,
Had a new power this Easter Day.
Not snatches of song but melody
Sustained and unified, ecstatic.
I could not hear the words and asked her,
'Ida, what is it you are singing?'

Her deep voice was bell-like with her joy
As she cried out for us all to hear,
'I'm singing to my Lord Jesus Christ!'
So, on Easter morning, he had come.
The great teapot became a Chalice
And the sugar basin a Paten.

The risen sun filled the ward with light,
We held out our hands for his bounty.

This poem first appeared in print in 1990 in an anthology of
Elizabeth's religious writing compiled by Christine Rawlins, entitled
A Vision of God.

How many people in that situation could put their own misery
and pain aside to understand that of others.

ELIZABETH GOUDGE IN 1974.
THE PHOTOGRAPH WAS USED IN THE FIRST EDITION OF *WEG* (NEW SCAN).

THE FIRST EDITION OF *A VISION OF GOD*

WRITING WITH A RELIGIOUS THEME

What do I believe about the vision of God, and about judgement? I believe
we are created by love and that sooner or later the persuasion of love will
draw us up out of our darkness to stand in the exquisite light and see
ourselves at last as we really are.

We have already seen how Elizabeth's books had made her readers aware of her faith and philosophy, even though she said it had been done unconsciously: 'In my case when a book comes into my mind it comes simply as a story—personal belief is something that comes in apparently without my knowledge or contriving.'

As her literary career advanced, her publishers possibly realised that many readers would welcome books written by her on specifically religious themes, and several of the books we look at in this chapter were the result of publishers proposing publishing this kind of work.

Before going on to these, it seems the most appropriate place to look at an earlier piece of writing that Elizabeth was asked to do.

During his lifetime Canon Goudge had written many books and essays on theology, and after his death a new collection of his essays was to be published under the title *Glorying in the Cross*. Elizabeth was asked to contribute a foreword to it, and wrote a detailed picture of his life from his early childhood in a strict Christian Evangelical home to his long career as a clergyman. He had gone up to Oxford in 1885 where he joined the Christian Union and made lifelong friends.

Although always loyal to the Church of England, he developed a distaste for protestant bigotry and intolerance, and these years saw the start of his interest in the ecumenical movement.

Both his parents died while he was at Oxford, which Elizabeth said left a streak of sadness in his make-up, although he considered cheerfulness as one of the first duties of a Christian, and his friends spoke of his sunny nature.

In 1889 he went to Wycliffe Hall, and after his ordination went as curate to St Mark's Church in Leicester. His only sister joined him there, helping with his ministry for the next four years. It was a working-class parish and Elizabeth said his gentleness endeared him to all the sick and old.

After this he joined the staff at Salisbury Cathedral for a year before joining the theological college at Wells as vice-principal. After eight years in that post, he was made principal and Elizabeth thought those sixteen years at Wells were the happiest in his life—teaching was his chief vocation and he had the backing of a splendid staff. She also remembered how vital he was in those days; his early delicacy left behind, he cycled, walked and played games. He hated slackness; mentally, spiritually, as well as physically he was always taut and vigorous and splendidly controlled. He had a temper but he kept it under iron control. To the end of his life he got up at 6.30 every morning and began each day with an hour's meditation and prayer. His concentration was immense; he could work or play with complete absorption, oblivious of time or place.

Neatness was characteristic of him—his handwriting, though not easy to read, was neat and precise. Although he loved good talk and entertaining, his shyness made him dislike society as such, and he didn't like being cluttered up with a lot of things; Elizabeth added that no man could have had fewer personal possessions. He was amazingly generous with everything he had—money, time or knowledge—and loved giving presents, but never gave them to himself. Prayer was the mainspring of his life, and he undertook no work in his life without praying about it.

Elizabeth also paid tribute to the lightness and gaiety which her mother had brought into her father's life, and the happiness they shared. He always read his latest writing or sermon to her and listened to her criticism, relying on her judgement and common sense.

A very strong trait in his character was his almost passionate love of the beauty of the world; country walks were his greatest joy—he was very knowledgeable about birds and butterflies.

While still at Wells, he was made a Doctor of Divinity, and soon after this came the move to Ely in 1911 and appointment to the canonry combined with the principalship of the theological college there. Through the years his views had been developing and his move was not altogether successful in accommodating them with those he now had to work with.

He continued with his writing and became noted as a man whose understanding of the Epistles excelled other theologians.

In the First World War, the theological college became a hospital and he took up the parish work in Ely and Wisbech of younger men who had gone to the front. He also worked as a night orderly in his old college.

During this time he contributed to a book called *The War and the Kingdom of God*, and found himself in some quarters branded as a pacifist. Years later he found himself branded as the opposite and was much amused, because his opinions had not changed. He later preached a sermon on this subject at Oxford, which was afterwards published and had a wide circulation.

After the war in 1921 he accepted a professorship of New Testament Interpretation at King's College London, where he stayed happily for two years, spending the week in London and weekends at Ely where he retained his canonry.

The move to Oxford in 1923 has already been covered in other parts of this book, but one comment Elizabeth made is worth recording, when she said, 'Gradually he seemed to find himself, he did not try to be anything but what he was, a churchman who was less interested in university affairs than in the affairs of the church at large, and as such he found his niche'. She also said that, as lecturing to diocesan clergy was also part of his work, he was delighted to hear he was called 'the parson's parson'.

A large part of his work was devoted to re-union, and he was on several committees and attended conferences both at home and abroad, wrote and pleaded for it in every possible way. He also worked with two colleagues to produce a *New Commentary on Holy Scripture*, with little financial reward.

A further interesting mention was of his love of letter writing— she said he always knew what he thought about everything, and his family, teasing him, would say that his first action to any turn of events was to seize his pen and write to *The Church Times*. His personal correspondence from all over the world was enormous, but he would never have a secretary or typewriter.

His leisure interests included play reading, chess, and crossword puzzles—detective stories and biographies were the only modern books of interest to him. Listening to Beethoven on his radio was another delight. But, said Elizabeth of her father, work was the best recreation of all, which is perhaps why he was afraid of feeling idle if he retired.

As we know, he worked until ten days before his death on April 24th, 1939, leaving Elizabeth to remember his last words, 'Dear one, it is loving that matters'.

I felt that this considerably condensed version of Elizabeth's foreword to her father's book should be included here for several reasons.

Elizabeth admitted that in her early childhood, she had been afraid of her father, and through much of her adult life she had felt in awe of his superior intellect. But she also wrote that she felt she had come very near to him at the end of his life, and part of her grief at his death was having no more time for that closeness to mature. Writing this very full account of his life must surely have helped her realise just how much she owed to him and how much he had helped her throughout her life, and it hopefully eased her grief.

Giving readers a better understanding of the background to her life as a clergyman's daughter makes it easier for us to realise how her knowledge of the Bible enabled her to quote so aptly from it in her writing.

Perhaps she didn't realise how much she took after her father in many respects. And in writing about his character traits, we learn more about Elizabeth as well. His influence on her later work was considerable.

The first collection of short stories with a religious theme was published in 1950 by her first publishers, Duckworth, and given the title of *The Reward of Faith and Other Stories*. It consisted of eight stories, with some like 'The Ikon on the Wall' previously published but with three new ones that Elizabeth wrote especially for the collection. This is how it was reviewed at the time: 'Each story told is of some manifestation of the triumph of the Christian faith in all lands and in all ages—that grain of mustard seed that has grown up to cover the whole earth, and as usual, the author is particularly charming when she makes a boy or girl the central character of her tales.'

In 1951, Hodder and Stoughton published Elizabeth's first specifically religious book, called *God So Loved the World*. It was dedicated to her four godchildren, and appears to be intended as a young person's guide to the life of Christ. While she was undoubtedly well versed to do it, only an experienced storyteller could have brought it to life, as though telling the story for the first time.

Elizabeth had never visited Israel, but just as she made New Zealand real to her readers in *Green Dolphin Country*, so she gave reality to the background of the life of Christ. As well as the narrative, Elizabeth also gave her thoughts on various parts of the story. About the Sermon on the Mount she wrote: 'If there was nothing at all to read in all the world but just this sermon, and all men read it and understood it, did it, then the Kingdom of God would come upon the earth in the following week.'

In the book's last chapter, called 'Victory', after recounting Christ's appearance to Mary after the Crucifixion, she wrote: 'Their own name spoken by a voice they love, can sometimes bring people back from unconsciousness, from near madness, even from the brink of death.'

Had this been her own experience whilst nursing her mother through her last difficult illness? The book was published in the same year that her mother had died.

Her next religious book was published by Duckworth in 1959.† The idea for a book on St Francis of Assisi had long been in her mind, and Franciscan theology had influenced her life and writing. Her father had also been an admirer of Francis, and she was possibly able to draw on some of his research and work as well as the books she acknowledged using.

Unable to undertake the journey to Assisi herself, she briefed Jessie Monroe to visit and to verify facts and obtain information for her book.

In her preface to the book Elizabeth wrote: 'Such a number of books have been written about Saint Francis, and so many of them works of scholarship, that a writer who is not a scholar should

† Published in the UK as *Saint Francis of Assisi* and in the USA as *My God and My All: The Life of Saint Francis of Assisi*. The latter title has since been used for a UK edition.

apologise for the presumption of attempting yet another. My only excuse is that I wanted to write it so much that I had to do so; my hope is that it may serve to introduce Saint Francis to a few who do not know him well and perhaps make them want to know him better.'

After her usual books, I have to admit I found this book hard going at the first reading, but the second time I found I was becoming more and more enthralled, not only about Francis's life, but in his band of followers as they tried to carry his message to other countries, including England, which I hadn't realised until then. I think others who, like me, had only known the usual stereotyped stories of the saint, would have found the book a revelation and a joy to read. From the beginning, right through to the end, Elizabeth conveyed the story in her own special way, as the following extract shows: 'It is never the beginning of a story to say a child is born, nor is it the end to say a man has died, for long preparation leads up to every birth, and death leaves behind it a power for good or evil that works on in the world for longer than the span of life from which it grew. In the case of those we call the saints, this power is immeasurable.

'Francis of Assisi is one of these. He lived eight centuries ago and died in middle age, yet few of us in the western world today, even if we know little about him, are not aware of him … his influence upon European music, art and drama, and politics, has been a study for many scholars. Yet it is as a Christian that he matters to us, as a humble poor man who set himself to tread as closely as he could in the footsteps of Christ, perhaps as closely as any man has ever done. Looking at him we see what it means to be a Christian, and what it costs. His story is not only endearing, it is terrifying.'

Elizabeth often said she did not find praying easy, and she was probably thinking of this as she wrote this about the followers of St Francis: 'Those who were beginners in prayer had to learn the hard way, through all the alternations of dryness, self disgust and shame, boredom, and hopelessness shot through with those moments of light that made it all worthwhile.'

Another small extract from her book shows the appeal the life of Francis would have had for her father: 'His greeting of "The Lord give thee peace," was no formal one. He cared passionately for peace, worked and prayed for it, primarily for the peace of God in the soul, but also for peace between nations and cities, and between one man and another.'

When writing the following passage, Elizabeth may have thought of her mother's psychic gifts that she mentioned in her autobiography: 'He [Francis] was not eager to heal, though he had the charismatic gift in high degree. He did not refuse, for healing the sick was a part of his apostolic obedience, but he would draw back from healing if he could do so without harshness ... the charismatic gift is a spectacular one, and he knew well that those who possess it must always be on their guard against spiritual pride.'

The book won the respect of even her most severe critics. She made no mention of it in her autobiography but hopefully the book's reception made her feel that it would have satisfied even her erudite father.

I feel slightly sad that Elizabeth had not been able to make the journey to Assisi. She never complained about the limitations caused by her arthritic condition, but wrote in her autobiography: 'We die with many places that we long to see unvisited. I have been luckier than most for many of the places that I longed to see, I have seen, but there are so many others I shall not see in this life. But as a ghost, perhaps? I hope so. And better that way for one would travel so light and miss the turmoil at the airports, and not get tired. And then there would be the extraordinary blessed loneliness of no one seeing you ...'

As far as I know, Elizabeth never experienced the hassle of air travel, but no doubt she had heard accounts from others. I like to think that she has now been given her 'private viewing' of the lovely country where Francis once walked.

In her book on Francis, Elizabeth used several quotations from the writings of the Italian Franciscan, Jacopone da Todi. She must have known about his life, for when she was once asked if she had known any saints, she appeared to consider him for that position, until she remembered he had not 'been raised to the altar' by his church because of his shocking temper.

I'm including the three poetry anthologies that Elizabeth compiled in this chapter, because although her choice of poems covered a very wide range, their titles, Comfort, Peace and Faith, suggest this is where they best belong.

Elizabeth's writing had always shown her love for and her extensive repertoire of poetry, so not surprisingly she was asked by the publishers at Michael Joseph to undertake the prodigious task of compiling an anthology on the subject of Comfort. I was told that she revelled in the work involved and the book was published in 1964, and stayed in print until a short time ago.

It is divided into five parts, with each part containing verse to appeal to all tastes. Elizabeth wrote this introduction which tells us much about her, as well as the work itself: 'There are few people who do not find their chief content in books. When we are lonely, ill, bereaved, afraid, it is almost always to a favourite book that we turn for comfort, and most of us also have our own private anthology that we carry about as part of the furniture of our mind; bits of poetry and prose that we have learnt over the years and repeat to ourselves during sleepless nights, in the dentist's waiting room or on the morning of the operation. But sometimes our memory does not function as well as usual, or we feel the need for something new, and it is then that we turn to someone else's anthology, a printed one, which differs only from the mental one in that there is more in it, because it contains not only all the compiler remembers but also all they would like to remember. This book, one sided and limited because conditioned by my ignorance and limitations, contains what I myself find comforting, and I am not only comforted by the great forms of the world, the glories of the Bible, and the remembrance of saints and heroes, though they are pre-eminent, but by comic rhymes, fairy tales, verse that set me remembering birds, bees and creatures of all sorts.'

Although Elizabeth possibly overestimated the number of people who shared her knowledge and appreciation of poetry, it was a great collection to dip into and must indeed have been a source of comfort and pleasure to many people.

In 1966 Hodder and Stoughton published a book of prayers collected and compiled by Elizabeth, given the title *A Diary of Prayer*. Correspondence between her and her publishers indicates that there was some difficulty in finding the authors of the prayers she had chosen in order to obtain copyright, with Elizabeth saying, 'during a lifetime of wide reading I picked up prayers here and there', but she had forgotten their source.

Where they were not successful in finding the author, the prayer is noted as 'anon.' However, this still leaves quite a number of prayers which appear to be her own and which give an indication of her prayer priorities.

A short preface written by Elizabeth for this book read: 'These prayers, a mixture of old and new, were not collected for literary merit, though some of the great prayers of the world are among them. If mistakes have been made we would ask forgiveness for this.' She was obviously concerned about not knowing the source of some of the prayers, but I don't imagine it really worried the people who bought the book. Of all her books, this, in my experience, is now the hardest one to come by, and it was only the loan of her copy from one of Elizabeth's friends that made it possible for me to see it.

The next book was a collection of stories around the theme of

Christmas, taken from novels Elizabeth had already written, with the addition of two new stories. *A Christmas Book* was published by Hodder and Stoughton in 1967, and no doubt solved many a problem as to what to give for a present that Christmas.

Elizabeth also wrote a preface for the book, in which she compared the pagan 'Feast of Lights' with the Christian festival and the festivities that had grown up around it, including the changes during her lifetime; but ended by saying they 'still continue to be reflections from the light that at the beginning of things moved upon the face of the waters'.

Following the success of *A Book of Comfort* Elizabeth was approached again by the publishers to compile another anthology, and in 1967 her *A Book of Peace* was in circulation.

She again wrote a preface which shows how profoundly she had approached the subject. She began: 'To be at peace. The longing for peace must have come with the dawn of reason as soon as man was able to ask of himself: What do I want?'

Again it was a carefully chosen selection, where in each group readers could find old favourites and yet be introduced to exciting new material. Elizabeth explained: 'The poems in this book are collected here simply because I love them all, but I have tried to arrange them in these four groups of natural beauty, peaceful work, love and home, and the mystery. So many things come under the last heading, dreams and myths and fairy tales, and the reverence and awe with which each one of us confront the mystery, and to which we give the odd name of religion. Only music, art and poetry can express our experience of mystery and then how inadequately ...'

Another collection of short stories was published by Hodder and Stoughton in 1971. It contained seven stories under the title of *The Lost Angel*, and of all seven, the story of 'The Lost Angel' is probably the best loved and remembered.

The book flap on my copy of *The Lost Angel* has four reviews of the book. The one I think summed it up best came from *Homes and Gardens* magazine: 'To all the charm and warmth and delight in the lovely things of life woven into this book, she has added a shining strand of the spiritual, and the real action is on that plane.'

In 1976, Hodder and Stoughton published a third anthology of poetry with the title *A Book of Faith*, for which Elizabeth wrote a foreword of three pages, which began: 'This book brings together some of the things that poets and writers have said about faith, not only faith itself, but about the people and things and experiences that can kindle faith.'

She also added a 'Compiler's Note' in which she wrote: 'The compiling of an anthology can be an act of thanksgiving. What would any of us do without the books and poems that help us along the way?—the books we return to again and again, the poems we learn by heart and repeat for comfort in sleepless nights?'

The anthology included work from many of the same authors as the two previous anthologies, including Shakespeare, John Donne, Robert Frost, Donald Swann, Norman Nicholson, Sydney Carter, Gerard Manley Hopkins, Ruth Pitter, Siegfried Sassoon, Edwin Muir, Leo Tolstoy, C. S. Lewis and many others.

My paperback copy of the book was published in 1989, which speaks for itself of its appeal for over thirteen years.

Elizabeth's habit of never putting the date of the year on her letters makes it difficult to know exactly when she was invited to contribute a script for the BBC to be broadcast in Holy Week, as mentioned in 'The Retirement Years',†† but it was probably the early seventies.

Her script began by reminding listeners of the link between the new life of spring and the Resurrection: 'Every year at this time,

†† There is no mention of a script in that chapter, although Sylvia Gower does refer to an 'earlier broadcast' at the BBC.

when the birds begin to sing and the crocuses are coming up like flames out of the earth, we come face to face with the astonishment of spring. There was not a trace of all this a short time ago; then there was darkness and cold and now there is singing and light. What has happened? Death has turned himself around, as the year has turned around, and shows us life, and this week we remember that God in the person of His son has also lived and died and risen again.'

She went on to talk about love and forgiveness from her own experience and finally about the importance to be able to accept forgiveness ourselves. She ended: 'Forgiveness is like spring. Flowing so freely to us from our Lord and God it is like sunshine and a west wind. It can make even our old age green and fresh.'

Finally, there are three books, compiled from Elizabeth's writing by three different people who, like me, wanted to make their contribution towards preserving her work and hopefully introducing it to new readers. Two of these were compiled during Elizabeth's lifetime and were published by Hodder and Stoughton.

Mary Baldwin compiled *The Ten Gifts*, which was published in 1969. She chose passages from Elizabeth's writing that illustrate ten qualities that appeared in her books. They were: Love, Wonder, Beauty, Delight, Compassion, Understanding, Faith, Tranquillity, Truth, Courage. Had she written the book after the publication of *The Child from the Sea*, an eleventh one would have needed to be added of Forgiveness, which Elizabeth said she rated the highest of all.

In her foreword Mary Baldwin wrote: 'The choice of selections for this anthology has been a mixture of delight and regret. Delight because the reading and rereading of Elizabeth Goudge's stories always reveals something fresh and stimulating. Regret, because from the abundance of materials so much has to be left out.'

The next book, extracting passages from Elizabeth's writing to accompany four headings, was compiled by Muriel Grainger in 1978. It was called *Pattern of People* and the four themes were:

Woven from the Past; A Chain of Children; Designs of the Heart; and Patchwork of Portraits.

I was especially interested to read how Muriel Grainger had succumbed to the appeal of Elizabeth's writing. This is how she said it happened: 'Hunting for holiday reading in a seaside newsagent, I found a shelf of Elizabeth Goudge's novels and chose *The Dean's Watch*. It captivated me completely and later on, when I had read many of her books, I wrote an article about this author and her unique gift of conveying to her readers the beauty and the mystery that are interwoven with our everyday lives.'

The third person, a lifelong lover of Elizabeth's writing, was Christine Rawlins, whose book *A Vision of God* was published in 1990 by Hodder and Stoughton (Spire). She also used passages from Elizabeth's books to show there were constant themes to be found within them, and she grouped these under four headings: 'I am the Light of the World'; 'I am the Way'; 'I am the Truth'; 'I am Life.'

Her book also included the poem 'Easter in the Ward', which Elizabeth wrote when she first went into hospital.

As I have explained in my introduction to this book, we have all been led in our various ways to try to share with others our conviction that Elizabeth's writing was unique, and to try to ensure her place amongst 20th-century women writers.

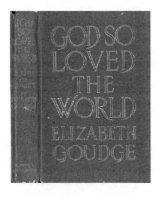

THE FIRST EDITION OF
GOD SO LOVED THE WORLD

THE FIRST EDITION OF *A BOOK OF FAITH*

ELIZABETH GOUDGE

ELIZABETH

THE PERSON

Elizabeth was often amused and slightly exasperated by the way her fans perceived her. Answering one rather effusive letter, she replied: 'It is lovely of you to think I am a saint. But here I have to contradict you absolutely—if you knew me really well what a terrible shock you would have.'

Sadly, there is only a small handful of people left who knew Elizabeth well, but they have all been generous in sharing their recollections of her with me. We have already heard their affirmation of her kindness and generosity; about her love for animals, birds, music, books, and the natural world.

The Joy of the Snow gave a wonderful glimpse into Elizabeth's life, but was, by her own admission, more the sharing of the happier memories from her long life than an autobiography. Her reticence and modesty wouldn't have allowed her to think anyone would be interested in any indulgence of self-analysis she might pass on to them.

Fortunately for those who think otherwise, there is another source which reveals more to us about her, and that is her books. Just as the sharing of her philosophy was done unconsciously, the same is true here, even though she claimed the opposite. Answering a question she often received from her readers, she wrote: 'Speaking for myself I do not put the woman I am into them, but after writing for years I noticed the regular appearance in story after story of a tall graceful woman, well balanced, intelligent, calm, capable and tactful. She is never flustered, forgetful, irritable or nervy. She does not drop bricks, say the opposite of what she means, let saucepans boil over or smash her best teapot. She is all I long to be and never will be. She is in complete reverse a portrait of myself.'

This is the nearest Elizabeth got to writing of how she perceived herself and is a joy to read. Some examples have already shown how, as in *The Scent of Water*, facets of her personality and habits would seem to be very similar to the characters she is writing about. Other, less obvious clues need closer scrutiny to give more information about her.

One of the American friends who visited Elizabeth in the early 1970s wrote about how she remembered her then: 'She wore a rose coloured dress belted at the waist ... I remember that Elizabeth Goudge's feet were long and elegant, and expensively shod.'

The books provide plenty of evidence that from childhood Elizabeth had been encouraged to care about her appearance, and that she had an awareness of fashion, for others, if not for herself. The description of the precocious Bella in *The Dean's Watch* appears to closely resemble the only photograph we have of Elizabeth as a young child (see page 257): 'She wore a starched muslin frock with short puffed sleeves and a frill round the neck. A blue sash encircled that part of her anatomy where in later years a waist would possibly develop, and her yellow curls were kept out of her eyes with a snood of blue ribbon.'

This is the kind of detailed description Elizabeth gave of all her feminine characters. There are several hints in *The Joy of the Snow* that Mrs Goudge was definitely fashion conscious and even if Elizabeth did not enjoy dressing for social occasions like her mother, she acquired a good taste in choosing clothes. The description of Nadine in *The Bird in the Tree* bears this out and is especially evocative of the thirties vogue in fashion: 'Her plain tweed coat and skirt, though ridiculously short, was superbly cut and of the loveliest shade of green imaginable, and the bright silk scarf knotted round her throat perfectly and exactly matched her lipstick. Nadine's shoes were green too … and her pearl earrings lustrous and very large.'

Elizabeth's upbringing also encouraged a love of beautiful things, and this combined with her studies at the Reading School of Art, where she was taught to observe things in minute detail such as 'the shape of a petal and the sheen of a bird's wing', made her appreciative of all forms of art and craft.

One of her treasured possessions was the collection of 'The Little Things' which she had inherited from her Guernsey grandmother. She described it in two of her books, *A City of Bells*, where it is owned by Mary at the sweetshop, and again in *The Scent of Water* where the owner is another Mary, who has inherited it from her cousin.

Visitors to Rose Cottage always remembered being shown the remarkable collection, which included 'tiny chairs carved out of ivory, a Bible the size of your thumbnail, a silk purse with tiny coins inside it, a teaset of Bristol china, a bottle of shells the size of pins' heads, a little telescope through which you could look and see a picture of Brighton, and many other treasures, thirty of them altogether, all of them works of art, and not a single one of them bigger than an acorn'.

Although she appreciated them, Elizabeth was never encouraged to be acquisitive of worldly goods, as the story in *The Joy of the Snow* shows when she is made to choose a basketful of her toys to give to poorer children in Wells. She had Henrietta and Hugh Anthony carry out the same charitable act in *A City of Bells*. This early training along with her compassionate nature probably accounts for her acts of generosity in later life that are so well remembered by so many people.

Many of the experiences that Elizabeth had happen in Henrietta's life in *A City of Bells* and in *Henrietta's House* seem very likely to be flashbacks to Elizabeth's own childhood in Wells. The disproportionate number of times that her various characters have to visit the dentist in her stories suggests that Henrietta's annual visit to the dentist in London was based on her own memories.

Like most children of her generation, Elizabeth would have been indulged with frequent visits to the sweetshop, like the one owned by the sisters Martha and Mary in Torminster, which was not exactly good for the teeth. Some of these children were less fortunate than others as to the damage caused, but her books would suggest that Elizabeth's teeth continued to be a source of trouble to her in later life.

In *A City of Bells* Grandfather Fordyce is very concerned for his two grandchildren as he takes them to the dentist: 'What would they not suffer before they reached that haven that he had now reached, that harbour of a top and bottom plate?'

Then there follows an account of Henrietta's ordeal: 'Without a word, and with the calm dignity of Mary Stuart on the scaffold, Henrietta removed her cap and muff and coat, climbed into the chair and opened her mouth ... "Shan't hurt you," said Mr Arbuthnot ... "A little wider please." But he did hurt. He hurt very much indeed. Three teeth did he fill and scraped off a lot of tartar, but Henrietta never moved or made a sound, though she felt pain more than most children, and felt, too, the awful indignity that it is to a woman to have a member of the opposite sex who is in no way related to her poking about in the inside of her mouth.

'"Teeth decay very easily," said Mr Arbuthnot in an undertone to Grandfather. "She'll have trouble later."' Whereas after Hugh Anthony's turn in the chair, Mr Arbuthnot reports, '"This fellow will never have much trouble ... Sound teeth. No nerves".'

When Elizabeth referred to herself as 'nervy', this was

undoubtedly true, as it is for many sensitive people, but as with her other problems of depression and later arthritis, she was never self-pitying about her adversities, using the experience to write more knowledgeably about characters in her stories suffering with similar problems.

How else could she have portrayed Jean Anderson in *The Scent of Water* so convincingly: 'The eyes, blue and beautiful, were not the eyes of the woman whom Jean appeared to be, and looking into them Mary was aware of intelligence and courage. She realised with deep respect that this woman had always done what she had to do and faced what she had to face. If many of her fears and burdens would have seemed unreal to another woman, there was nothing unreal about her courage.'

In *The Rosemary Tree* she was able to write convincingly about the Wentworths' ex-housekeeper, Harriet, now confined to her room with arthritis, and finding her feeling of uselessness more difficult to bear than the pain of her condition.

None of these characters was depicted as one to be pitied, showing instead the strengths that could be won through affliction.

I learnt from one of Elizabeth's American correspondents that her knowledge of Elizabeth's bouts of depression gleaned from reading her books had helped her accept her own mood swings, which until then, neither she nor her family had really understood.

Even without experiencing extreme depression, very few people go through life without something akin to Grandfather Fordyce's experience: 'There had come to him one of those moments of quiet despair that lie in wait for even the happiest. Stealthy-footed they leap upon us, as we walk along the street, as we sit at evening with fruit and wine upon the table and laughter on our lips, as we wake suddenly from sleep in the hour before dawn; neither at our work nor our play nor our prayers are we safe, those moments can leap at any time out of the blackness around human life and suddenly the colours that we have nailed to our mast are there no longer and all that we have grasped is dust.'

I've found that some readers find it hard to believe Elizabeth could have remembered so much from her past to use in her writing. Here is perhaps an explanation to account for that gift: Jocelyn says to Henrietta, 'What a memory you have got,' to which Henrietta replies, 'I remember things that I like. They go in my eyes or my ears and down inside and stay there.'

Another piece attributed to Henrietta shows how early in her life Elizabeth discovered that literature was to be one of her main interests: 'Henrietta loved words, both the shape and the sound of them ... [and] she had discovered through words the symbolism of sound and shape and their relationship ... "Silver" was a word that she especially loved ... because it was so cool ... it was a satisfactory word to write too, with its capital S flowing like a river, its I tall as a silver spear and the V like an arrow-head upside down. Yellow was another good word because of that glorious capital Y that was like a man standing on a mountain-top at dawn praying to God, with his arms stretched out, his figure black against a sky the colour of buttercups ... All her life yellow was her favourite colour and the one that symbolised the divine to her.'

Whether yellow was Elizabeth's favourite colour I don't know, but I do know that one of the visitors to Rose Cottage remembered her surprise at finding the entrance door painted a bright yellow.

Another notion some readers seem to have is that Elizabeth was a lonely person. The only time that Elizabeth admitted to such a feeling was in her childhood when her first playmates moved away from Wells, but that was soon compensated by other interests. I find that those of a gregarious nature often assume that more solitary people must be lonely. This is often far from true, and following Elizabeth's life story, I'm sure she would not have regarded herself in this way—apart from being very much 'a family person', her imaginative mind would make it unlikely. There are no characters in her books that are portrayed as lonely, if one excepts Sebastian in *The Heart of the Family*, and he was desolated by the loss of his family, rather than lonely in the accepted sense. Time to herself was essential, as was shown when she was writing of the Oxford years, and the places she found where she could be alone.

Writing in *The Joy of the Snow*, Elizabeth wrote: 'My mother's illness had troubled me all my life, and I felt guilty as well as unhappy.' This makes me think what I was told regarding Mrs Goudge's illness, although hard to understand, must be true. The story goes that Nanny had told Elizabeth that it was her birth that was responsible for her mother's illness. This was hardly the whole story, and was a cruel thing with which to burden a small child. There seems little doubt that it was more the cycling accident during pregnancy that was the real cause, even if in turn the injuries may have complicated the birth. It probably just slipped out when Nanny was cross, but it was not something Elizabeth would easily forget.

As with all mother-daughter relationships, there were probably times when Mrs Goudge appeared autocratic and demanding, especially during the wartime years in Devon, when for the first time Mrs Goudge had neither nanny nor maid to call on. Elizabeth had the household to practically run on her own in addition to her writing.

The nearest Elizabeth ever got to admitting the problem was in comparing her mother to the character of Lucilla in the Eliot books. Whatever her other inestimable qualities, Lucilla expected to have her own way, and this was probably equally true of Mrs Goudge. Elizabeth's relationship with her father, though always loving, was somewhat tinged with awe by his accomplishments, maybe giving her an inferiority complex as to her own gifts. They had drawn nearer to each other during his last years, and he certainly influenced her writing considerably after his death.

The female influence of mother, nanny, aunts, and school

teachers, seems to have made her portray the female characters in her stories as being more powerful than the men, but there was nothing to suggest that feminism played any part in her thinking. In the portrayal of young boys such as Hugh Anthony, Tommy, and Richard in *The Child from the Sea*, she seems to go along with the idea of male chauvinism, which was very much the accepted norm until the outbreak of the Second World War.

Elizabeth's ability to empathise with the difficulties brought on by old age must have been engendered by her own grandparents and the elderly people she met through her father's ministry. This resulted, while she herself was still comparatively young, in being able to write about older characters unusually well—Miss Montague in *The Dean's Watch* perhaps being the most memorable.

Although for much of her life, Elizabeth's situation meant that food 'appeared' rather than had to be dwelt on, the few references to it would seem to indicate that it did not have a very high priority in her life. There is a mention in *The Rosemary Tree* of a simple meal shared by Miss Wentworth, John and Michael, which may signify that the presentation of a meal was as important to her as the content: '... Miss Wentworth, who for some reason or other had replaced her hat, helped the broccoli gratin out of a Staffordshire dish while John poured the wine from the cobwebbed old bottle into exquisite goblets of amber-coloured glass. There were daffodils in a Spode mug. There was a large brown loaf on the table in a pewter dish, biscuits in a posset pot of Bristol Delft, apples in a bowl of white jade and a strong brew of black coffee in a Lowestoft jug.'

Did Elizabeth keep abreast of world affairs? Probably more in her retirement years, when there was more time to listen to radio and television as well as reading newspapers. Again I could not find much reference to her characters' interest in this field, except when Daphne Wentworth in *The Rosemary Tree* said, 'John and I never read the paper thoroughly. John is too conscientious to be headline-minded. He reads *The Times* leading article slowly and repeatedly until he has understood every word, but that's all he has time for. I read headlines only, and if the children are ill I don't read even those.'

However, remarks to friends in her letters show Elizabeth did feel great concern for troublesome events both at home and abroad.

To sum up what her writing reveals about Elizabeth, we can look at the analysis of it by Mary Baldwin in her book *The Ten Gifts*. She showed how ten qualities in life appeared constantly throughout Elizabeth's writing: Love, Wonder, Beauty, Delight, Compassion, Understanding, Faith, Tranquillity, Truth and Courage.

Surely, if the good fairies bestowed gifts on Elizabeth, it was the same things they wished for her.

All frail human beings struggle with the misfortunes dealt out that prevent them reaching their potential. Elizabeth had her share of these, as we know, but managed to win through and in her writing, give others the chance to recognise those qualities which had become part of her way of life.

ELIZABETH GOUDGE AS A YOUNG CHILD (USED IN THE FIRST EDITION OF *WEG*, NEW SCAN)

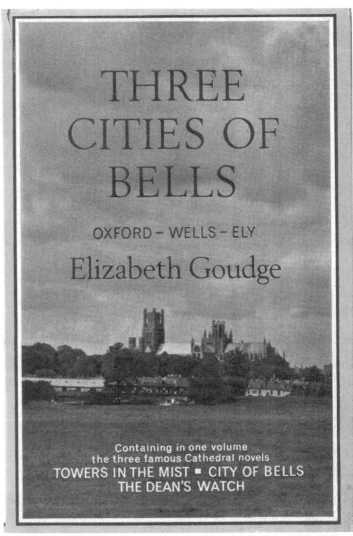

THREE
CITIES OF
BELLS

OXFORD – WELLS – ELY

Elizabeth Goudge

Containing in one volume
the three famous Cathedral novels
TOWERS IN THE MIST ■ CITY OF BELLS
THE DEAN'S WATCH

THE FIRST EDITION OF THE OMNIBUS, *THREE CITIES OF BELLS*

ELIZABETH GOUDGE 1900–1984

Island Magic—Duckworth 1934
The Middle Window—Duckworth 1935
A City of Bells—Duckworth 1936
A Pedlar's Pack and Other Stories—Duckworth 1937
Towers in the Mist—Duckworth 1938
Three Plays: Suomi, The Brontës of Haworth, Fanny Burney—Duckworth 1939
The Sister of the Angels. A Christmas Story—Duckworth 1939
The Bird in the Tree—Duckworth 1940
Smoky-House—Duckworth 1940
The Golden Skylark and Other Stories—Duckworth 1941
The Castle on the Hill—Duckworth 1942
Henrietta's House—University of London Press 1942
The Ikon on the Wall, and Other Stories—Duckworth 1943
Green Dolphin Country—Hodder & Stoughton 1944
The Little White Horse—University of London Press 1946
At the Sign of the Dolphin: An Elizabeth Goudge Anthology—Hodder & Stoughton 1947
The Herb of Grace—Hodder & Stoughton 1948
Make-Believe—Duckworth 1949
Gentian Hill—Hodder & Stoughton 1949
The Reward of Faith and Other Stories—Duckworth 1950
God So Loved the World—Hodder & Stoughton 1951
The Valley of Song—University of London Press 1951
White Wings: Collected Short Stories—Duckworth 1952

The Heart of the Family—Duckworth 1953
The Rosemary Tree—Hodder & Stoughton 1956
The White Witch—Hodder & Stoughton 1958
Saint Francis of Assisi—Duckworth 1959
The Dean's Watch—Hodder & Stoughton 1960
The Scent of Water—Hodder & Stoughton 1963
Linnets and Valerians—Leicester, Brockhampton Press 1964
A Christmas Book—Hodder & Stoughton 1967
I Saw Three Ships—Leicester, Brockhampton Press 1969
The Child from the Sea—Hodder & Stoughton 1970
The Lost Angel—Hodder & Stoughton 1971
The Joy of the Snow: An Autobiography—Hodder & Stoughton 1974

Collections:
The Eliots of Damerosehay—Hodder & Stoughton 1957 (including *The Bird in the Tree, The Herb of Grace, The Heart of the Family*)
Three Cities of Bells—Hodder & Stoughton 1965 (including *Towers in the Mist, A City of Bells, The Dean's Watch*)
The Ten Gifts (edited by Mary Baldwin)—Hodder & Stoughton 1969
Pattern of People (edited by Muriel Grainger)—Hodder & Stoughton 1978

Anthologies edited by Elizabeth Goudge:
A Book of Comfort—M. Joseph 1964
A Diary of Prayer—Hodder & Stoughton 1966
A Book of Peace—M. Joseph 1967
A Book of Faith—Hodder & Stoughton 1976

All above books were also printed in the USA by Coward-McCann.

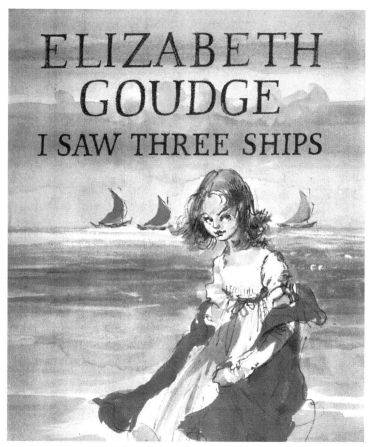

THE FIRST EDITION OF *I SAW THREE SHIPS*—THE SEA IS CONTINUED ON THE
BACK COVER, BUT HAS NO OTHER ILLUSTRATION

THE FIRST EDITION OF *The Well of the Star*

BOOKS BY ELIZABETH GOUDGE

Novels
Island Magic—Duckworth 1934
The Middle Window—Duckworth 1935
A City of Bells—Duckworth 1936
Towers in the Mist—Duckworth 1938
The Bird in the Tree—Duckworth 1940
The Castle on the Hill—Duckworth 1942
Green Dolphin Country—Hodder & Stoughton 1944 (US title *Green Dolphin Street*) (filmed as *Green Dolphin Street* 1947)
The Herb of Grace—Hodder & Stoughton 1948 (US title *Pilgrim's Inn*)
Gentian Hill—Hodder & Stoughton 1949
The Heart of the Family—Duckworth 1953
The Rosemary Tree—Hodder & Stoughton 1956
The White Witch—Hodder & Stoughton 1958
The Dean's Watch—Hodder & Stoughton 1960
The Scent of Water—Hodder & Stoughton 1963
The Child from the Sea—Hodder & Stoughton 1970

Omnibus Collections
The Eliots of Damerosehay—Hodder & Stoughton 1957 (including *The Bird in the Tree, The Herb of Grace, The Heart of the Family*)
Three Cities of Bells—Hodder & Stoughton 1965 (including *Towers in the Mist, A City of Bells, The Dean's Watch*)

A Story by

E L I Z A B E T H   G O U D G E

The Shufflewing

with pictures by

I S A B E L   M O R T O N - S A L E

THE FIRST EDITION OF *THE SHUFFLEWING*

Children's Books
The Sister of the Angels. A Christmas Story—Duckworth 1939
Smoky-House—Duckworth 1940
Henrietta's House—University of London Press 1942 (US title *The Blue Hills*)
The Little White Horse—University of London Press 1946 (filmed as a TV series, *Moonacre* 1994, and as a film, *The Secret of Moonacre* 2008)
Make-Believe—Duckworth 1949
The Valley of Song—University of London Press 1951
Linnets and Valerians—Leicester, Brockhampton Press 1964 (also published as *The Runaways*)
I Saw Three Ships—Leicester, Brockhampton Press 1969

Pamphlets, with illustrations by Isabel Morton-Sale
Maria or The Good Little Girl—Devon, Parnassus Books 1964
Arabella or The Bad Little Girl—Devon, Parnassus Books 1964
Serena the Hen—Devon, Parnassus Books 1964
The Shufflewing—Devon, Parnassus Books 1964

Short Stories (not including Religious Short Stories)
The Fairies' Baby and Other Stories—W. & G. Foyle 1919
A Pedlar's Pack and Other Stories—Duckworth 1937
The Golden Skylark and Other Stories—Duckworth 1941
The Well of the Star—Coward-McCann 1941 (US only)
White Wings: Collected Short Stories—Duckworth 1952

Religious Books (including Religious Short Stories)
The Ikon on the Wall and Other Stories—Duckworth 1943
The Reward of Faith and Other Stories—Duckworth 1950
David the Shepherd Boy (short story in Advent calendar format, illustrated by B. Biro)—Hamish Hamilton c1950
God So Loved the World—Hodder & Stoughton 1951

Saint Francis of Assisi—Duckworth 1959 (US title and also published in the UK as *My God and My All: The Life of Saint Francis of Assisi*)
The Lost Angel: Stories (with illustrations by Shirley Hughes)—Hodder & Stoughton 1971

Anthologies edited by Elizabeth Goudge
A Book of Comfort—M. Joseph 1964
A Diary of Prayer—Hodder & Stoughton 1966
A Book of Peace—M. Joseph 1967
A Christmas Book (extracts from her own novels)—Hodder & Stoughton 1967
A Book of Faith—Hodder & Stoughton 1976

Anthologies edited by Others
The Elizabeth Goudge Reader (edited by Rose Dobbs)—Coward-McCann 1946 (published in the UK as *At the Sign of the Dolphin: An Elizabeth Goudge Anthology*—Hodder & Stoughton 1947)
The Ten Gifts (edited by Mary Baldwin)—Hodder & Stoughton 1969
Pattern of People (edited by Muriel Grainger)—Hodder & Stoughton 1978
A Vision of God (edited by Christine Rawlins)—Hodder & Stoughton (Spire) 1990

Plays
Three Plays: Suomi, The Brontës of Haworth, Fanny Burney—Duckworth 1939

Autobiography
The Joy of the Snow: An Autobiography—Hodder & Stoughton 1974

Other
'My Father', preface to *Glorying in the Cross* by H.L. Goudge—Hodder & Stoughton 1940

Songs and Verses—Duckworth 1947
The Chapel of the Blessed Virgin Mary, Buckler's Hard, Beaulieu—Kings
of Lymington c1958
Publicity paragraph on the dustjacket of *The Rider of the White Horse*
(1959) and *Sword at Sunset* (1963), by Rosemary Sutcliff

Most of the above books were also printed in the USA by Coward-
McCann.

THE FIRST EDITION OF *MAKE-BELIEVE* (SEE PAGES 43 AND 136)

THE FIRST AMERICAN EDITION OF *THE GOLDEN SKYLARK*

ACKNOWLEDGEMENTS

I would like to thank all the people who have encouraged me to write this book.

Thanks to all local publications which have provided me with information.

Thank you to the staff of The Priaulx Library in Guernsey and staff of other libraries in the UK who have given me help.

Thanks to Kathleen Millington for all her help and encouragement, and to Jessie Monroe and Mark and Liz Dutton for help with my research.

Warm thanks to Dr Kate Lindemann and Elizabeth's friends in the USA for sharing their memories of Elizabeth.

To Anna Rashbrook, for her generous help.

To Shirley Stainer and my patient husband who have helped in transporting me to the places where Elizabeth lived.

I am also grateful to David Higham Associates and the estate of Elizabeth Goudge for permission to include extracts from Elizabeth Goudge's books and from her unpublished correspondence.

Sylvia Gower
Mersea Island
December 2001

THE FIRST EDITION OF *A CHRISTMAS BOOK*

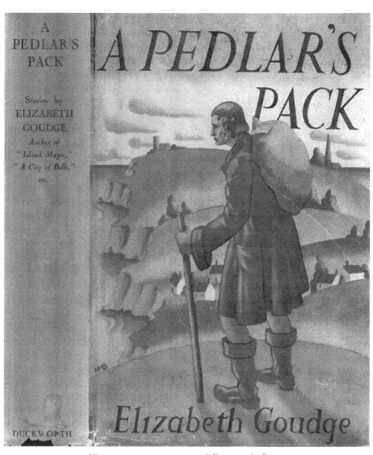

THE FIRST EDITION OF *A PEDLAR'S PACK*

GIRLS GONE BY PUBLISHERS

Girls Gone By Publishers republish some of the most popular children's fiction from the 20th century, concentrating on those titles which are most sought after and difficult to find on the second-hand market. Our aim is to make them available at affordable prices, and to make ownership possible not only for existing collectors but also for new ones, so that the books continue to survive.

We also publish some new titles which fit into the genre, including our Chalet School fill-ins, all professionally edited. Authors on the GGBP fiction list include Helen Barber, Elinor Brent-Dyer, Monica Edwards, Josephine Elder, Antonia Forest, Elizabeth Goudge, Phyllis Matthewman, Malcolm Saville, Jane Shaw and Lisa Townsend.

We also publish non-fiction titles, currently including *The Encyclopaedia of Girls' School Stories* (in three volumes) by Sue Sims and Hilary Clare. The non-fiction books are in a larger format than our fiction, and they are lavishly illustrated in black and white.

For details of availability and when to order, see our website or write for a catalogue to GGBP, The Vicarage, Church Street, Coleford, Radstock, Somerset, BA3 5NG, UK

https://www.ggbp.co.uk/